1

Hitting Drills

and
Much More

Blue Marble

We have not been thrown
out of the garden
but into it to enjoy the beauty of life.
Where else would you find
a blue marble in the vastness of space
growing food right out
of the ground?

Hitting Drills and

Much More

Designed By

Robert M. Braun, Sr.

Edited by

Mary L. Maffei

Mary states: I ensure that every individual that I encounter, is always treated with dignity and respect.

Edited by: Mary L. Maffei

Because of the dynamic nature of the Internet, any web addresses or links contained in this book may have changed since publication and may no longer be valid. The views expressed in this work are solely those of the author and do not necessarily reflect the views of the publisher, editors, and the publisher hereby disclaims any responsibility for them.
Printed in the United States of America.

ISBN: 978-1-890007-30-0 (sc)

Library of Congress Control Number:

Requests for permission to make copies of any part of this work should be mailed to: Permissions Department, River Magic Publishing,
P.O. Box #8, Titusville, NJ 08560.
Email: Rivermagic10@gmail.com.

This Book Belongs To:_____

COVER BY D BRAUN
ON DECK (1993, color pencil, 10" x 14")
The "On Deck" drawing is a young baseball player waiting for his time to hit.
With the sharp edges of the dugout in the background and the fence in front, the
on-deck hitter stands out. At this moment a hitter must have confidence in
themself. Confidence comes from working hard and smart.

Hitting Drills
and
Much More

Written By:
Steve R. Braun

Richard J. Braun

Robert M Braun, Sr

Illustrated By:
Richard J. Braun

To our children and grandchildren.

Table of Contents

..

Introduction

This hitting drill book is designed to help correct many common hitting mistakes like stepping in the bucket, casting, and many others. It also provides valuable information regarding the development and management of ball players. From the simple task of choosing the right bat to the ultimate ingredients for hitting success, all the way to hitting drills. It is simple enough for a new player, and sophisticated enough for the most advanced player. It is a usable tool for the first-year coach to the seasoned veteran. All can benefit by reading and using many of the ideas and drills shown in the book.

It's so easy for hitters to fall into bad habits and these bad habits can be corrected only by repeating the correct hitting mechanics demonstrated. When performing these drills, it is extremely important that each drill be performed correctly since research has shown that it takes seventeen (17) correct muscle movements to correct one (1) wrong movement. Therefore, the earlier the correct muscle movement can be programmed into the brain, the easier it will be to become a good hitter.

Hopefully, this book will fill a void in the basic baseball skill development market. When searching for instructional books in libraries and book stores very few were found. Most baseball books are about present or past professional baseball players; most are great stories but few provide the necessary instructions for the development of ball players and managers.

Chapter 1 – *The Art of Coaching* – is a collection of short articles by Bob published in a newsletter. Each is designed to help get the most out of each player.

Chapter 2 – *Bat Selection* – explains how to choose the correct bat. It explains why there are different types of bats, gives a method on how to determine the correct weight bat, and how to deal with wooden bats when reaching pro ball.

Chapter 3 – *Grip* – gives examples of the best method to hold a bat and how much grip pressure should be applied when hitting.

Chapter 4 – *Plate coverage* – explains why it is so important to get into the same spot in the batter box every time, and explains how to use the bat as a measuring tool.

Chapter 5 – *Strike Zone Discipline* – explains why the hitter should swing at strikes.

Chapter 6 – *Ultimate Ingredients for Hitting Success* – Deals with the recipe of ingredients from desire to visual reminders that are necessary to help develop a good mental approach towards becoming a good hitter.

Chapter 7 – *Basic Offensive Strategy* – Emphasizes the need and reasons for a total team effort and responsibilities needed by each player to score runs and win ball games.

Chapter 8 – *Basic Hitting Philosophy* – Deals with the interaction of swing mechanics, concentration, confidence, and strike zone discipline, how they work together and basic goals every hitter should have.

Chapter 9 – *Hitting Philosophies & Theories* – Deals with working on muscle memory and working to be a good hitter.

Chapter 10 – *Mental Skills for Hitters* – Explains the importance of the mental side of hitting, taking mental inventory, active awareness, and reframing.

Chapter 11 – *Running a good Practice* – Gives examples of good practice routines, infield and bunting drills, and advanced hitting routine.

Chapter 12 – *Situation Hitting* – Gives the Offensive strategies for different situations like what to do with runner held at first, lead-off hitter in the game, runner on third less than two outs, and more. This chapter is designed to coordinate the offensive strategy of both manager and players.

Chapter 13 – *Hitting Drills* – forty-five (45) different hitting drills designed to help correct hitting mistakes like stepping into the bucket, casting, and many more.

Chapter 14 - *Baseball Statistics* – Provides basic statistics used to evaluate players and team.

Chapter 15 - *"Becoming a Pro"* – Steve Braun Pinch-hitter deluxe, Doctor Stroke.

Chapter 16 - *The Brothers' Story* – All three were successful: Steve in Baseball, Richard in Art, and Bob in Writing.

The Art of Coaching

Manager Whity Herzog and player Steve Braun became great
friends during the time Steve played and coached for Whity.
Steve helped Whity win the 1982 World Series.
Pencil drawing by Rich Braun

The following is a selection of articles by Bob published in sports newsletters which are designed to help coaches and all of us become better. Most of the articles are directed to the development of the next generation, our future. We must all take the time to learn a healthier way, both mentally and physically in rearing our children, and taking control of our lives. Take the time to read the following articles. They may point you in the right direction or just reinforce what you are already doing.

Art of Coaching 1
By Bob Braun

Many years ago, when learning the game of baseball, I can remember my father telling my brothers and me, that the most important job of a coach is getting the most out of each player. With that philosophy, the success of a coach's ability is not measured by win/loss record; it's measured by how much improvement each player makes during the season.

This philosophy translates into more than hoping a young player improves. It means spending time with your players at practice and emphasizing that the game is played not just to win but also for fun. It means continually gaining knowledge and improving as a coach. Practice should include drills that keep every player moving and involved. Words of encouragement and praise should be given even if mistakes are made. Always look for the positive and build from there.

If young players feel good about themselves, they are willing to learn. Their play will improve as confidence increases. It is important that confidence be built at an early age, so a coach should always balance playing time and position with ability. Let the young player improve and grow before placing them in critical positions like pitcher, catcher, shortstop, or first base. Remember, you are building a person so be patient, work hard, and always give words of encouragement. Make the game fun for both you, and your players.

Art of Coaching 2
By Bob Braun

The ability to get your message across is vital. If you can't communicate your instructions and ideas to your players you will not succeed as a coach. Bob Boone said, when accepting the manager's position of the Kansas City Royals, "What a teacher needs is a student. What a student needs, is to know that they want to learn about what you know. The key is establishing a relationship."

Getting close to your players and giving them training tools to help you convey your message is the key to coaching success. It is easier if you and the players are on the same plane. Use any tool to get your message across. If it's a video, study it yourself then give it to your players. This will help you both understand what is being taught and what needs to be learned.

Establish a friendship with your players. Make an effort to help them improve both mentally and physically. Always make them feel good about themselves. But, you can't let them walk over you so you must maintain control by making sure everyone knows who's in charge. Enjoy your responsibilities as a coach and continue to make an effort to do your best. You will be rewarded by knowing you are helping your players mature into responsible adults.

Art of Coaching 3
By Bob Braun

In the past, I've expressed the importance of getting the most out of each player, how a coach should instill confidence, and that the amount of improvement of each player is the measurement of coaching success. The coach's knowledge of baseball and his skills to convey this knowledge to the players must also be developed.

In the forty-plus years that I've been involved with baseball, I've seen great players that were not good coaches and mediocre players that were great coaches. It's important to know baseball but it's more important to be able to transfer your knowledge. It takes a fine blend of control, confidence, friendship, leadership, and energy.

Control, in that kids look up to someone who is in control and has confidence in the knowledge they are receiving. Friendship comes by getting to know each player's personality, athletic skills, and weaknesses so that the best method can be used to get your message across. Leadership is obtained by running organized practices where everyone is involved and making the correct decisions during a game. Energy is used by being involved and giving encouragement during the entire practice or game.

Take pride in your leadership role and continue to strive to gather more knowledge about the game through books, clinics, videos, observation of other coaches or simply playing baseball yourself. Remember, you're not only molding yourself into a caring, concerned person, you're setting an example for tomorrow's future.

Art of Coaching 4
By Bob Braun

Greatness just does not happen. It takes a fine blend of natural talent, desire to be the best, and what I call, coachability. Natural talent plays a big part in determining the eventual level one will obtain but it's only a part of the formula of greatness. Obviously, it helps to be tall, quick, and able to jump to be a great basketball player. Good eye-hand coordination and quick reflexes are necessary to hit a ninety (90) miles-per-hour fast ball. A finely tuned ear is a must to be a musician. All great individuals have been blessed with some sort of physical natural talent but, many do not reach greatness, even though they have talent.

The desire to be the best will propel one beyond what natural talent will do by itself. This desire will stimulate the need to practice and help focus the need. As one improves and receives enjoyment in feeling successful, the need to work harder will be created. As the need to work harder increases more time, both mentally and physically, will be spent to improve. With more time, the improvement quickens.

Soon you have a person that not only understands the importance of listening but also can apply the instructions they receive. They are coachable.

Greatness can be achieved and comes in many forms. It is the responsibility of all coaches, parent, grandparents, teachers, and anyone training our youth to stimulate the desire to be the best they can be. Encouragement, praise, and discipline, plus learning to work hard plays a big part. Always keep in mind that you are dealing with our future and the better our children become, the better our future will be.

Bob coaching his grandson Andrew
as the third base coach.

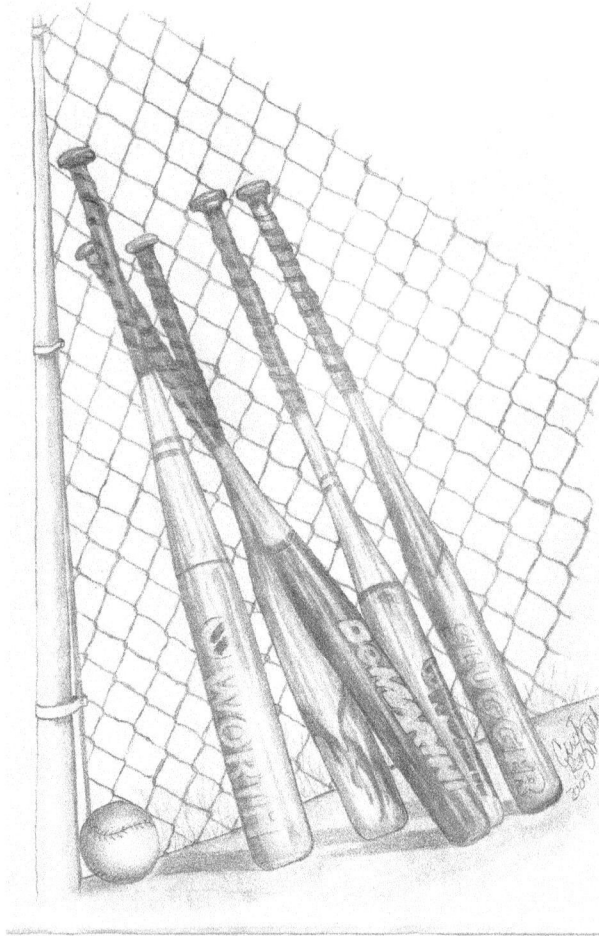

Bat Selection

Physical characteristics differ from player to player. That's the reason there are many different models of bats. It is important to find a bat that is comfortable and fits the hitting style being used. At one time almost all hitters used heavy bats. Today, hitters have a great variety from which to choose. So, experiment and choose a bat most comfortable for you.

One thing to keep in mind while choosing a bat is hand size. If the hands are small you should not get a bat with a real thick handle. Gripping a bat properly with small hands and a thick handle can be a problem.

But speed and quickness are important, especially in the rotation hitting style. If you basically use this hitting style, you may consider using a light bat with a thin handle. This type gives you greater quickness and bat speed. It can give you a feeling of whipping the bat with your hands not your body. If the bat is too heavy, you can lose the whipping feel, but be careful about using one that is too light. If it is too light the ball will not jump off the bat with as much velocity. So, find a happy medium.

Players using the weight shift hitting style may choose to go to a little heavier bat. In using this style, the hitter is using less snapping or whipping of the hands and more of a pulling action of the lead arm.

Any size bat or model will work with any hitting style, but there are some common factors that make sense. The most important thing when choosing a bat is that the bat feels comfortable. A good way to determine the proper weight is, by holding the bat with the left hand if hitting from the right side, and your right hand if hitting left-handed, with the pinkie hanging over the end of the bat. With the raised and elbow straight, raise the bat. If the elbow must be bent to raise the bat then the bat is too heavy.

Most hitters haven't been exposed to a large variety of wood bat models. A good time to experiment is when you first get into pro ball. There are usually lots of different models around most clubhouses. Also, when experimenting with these new bats seek the advice of one of the hitting instructors. They have seen many models over their careers and can be very helpful in this area.

Another thing to remember when using a wooden bat, (not a factor when using the aluminum bat) the label is either held up facing the hitter or down facing the ground. This lines up the grain of the bat properly. If it is held with the label either facing the pitcher or facing the catcher it isn't as strong and will break easily.

The label is either held up facing the hitter or down facing the ground.
Facing the hitter is preferred.

Grip

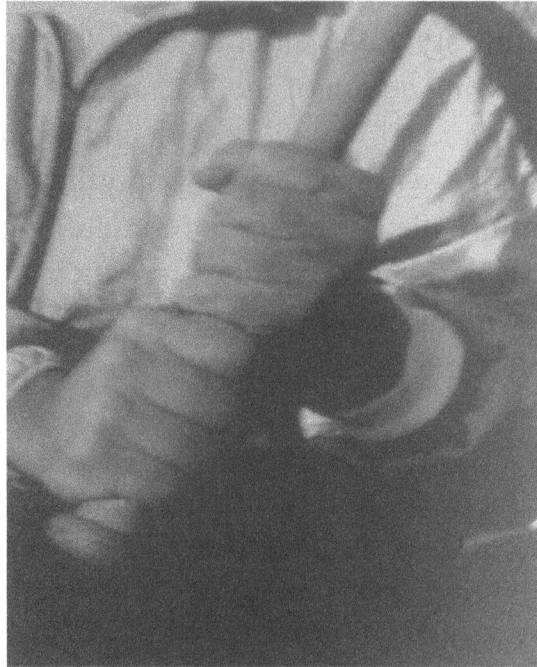

Your grip should be firm but, also be relaxed and comfortable.

There are three basic ways the bat can be held. One of the three ways gives the hitter an advantage. The three ways are:

1) Deep in the palm or choked.

2) Higher up in the fingers.

3) Where the fingers meet the palms.

There are disadvantages in grips 1 and 2 and the most advantage is grip 3. The disadvantage to grip 1 is it puts the bat so far back in the palm that the finger tips do not provide enough contact with the bat. This greater sense of feel of grip 3 gives the hitter greater control of the bat.

It is similar to the surgeon when he holds the scalpel, he holds it in his fingertips. This gives him a great sense of feel and control; the instrument can be maneuvered precisely. Would you have surgery done by a surgeon who choked his scalpel?

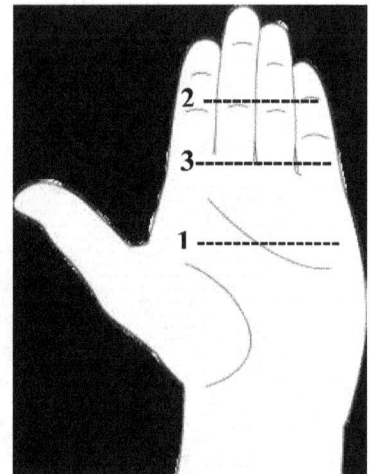

Grip 2 puts the bat more in the fingers. Holding the bat this way takes the bat almost completely out of the palm, which is the strongest part of the hand.

When the hitter puts the bat only in the fingers, he loses stability and control. Holding the bat where the thumb pad meets the palm gives the bat stability. At the point of contact the hitter is redirecting the great force created by the mass of the thrown ball. If the bat isn't stable, the bat would almost be knocked out of the hitter's hands.

The most desirable grip is grip 3. This grip allows the fingertips to have enough contact with the bat. It also gives enough stability because the bat has contact where the thumb pad meets the palm.

Again, it's important to experiment with different handle thicknesses. Put the handle in the areas described and feel the difference in each grip. Think about the advantages and disadvantages.

Another important point to remember, hitters who use the choking grip (grip 1) sometimes also wrap their top hand all the way around the bat with the knuckles facing the pitcher. This hand position puts the thumb pad of the top hand under the bat instead of behind it at contact. This is a very weak position. Putting the hand behind the bat helps absorb the shock of the pitched ball. Also, holding the bat this way can limit top hand extension, because the wrist is cocked inwardly instead of outwardly. This inward hand position will cause the bat to start up and out of the strike zone too soon, rather than staying down and through.

Also, important is how much grip pressure you apply to the handle. Again, the hitter has an advantage if he chooses the middle ground, not too tight but not too loose. Holding the bat too tight causes the forearms to tighten. This restricts the hand action which causes the swing to be slower. This especially affects the quickness needed for the rotation hitting style.

Holding the bat too loosely can cause the hitter to lose a sense of aggressiveness. Also, he/she can lose bat stability. Strive for a grip that is in between the two extremes.

Another grip which has become popular is putting the little finger of the bottom hand over the knob. This grip is strongly discouraged because of the large number of injuries to a small bone in the hand.

PLATE COVERAGE

Plate coverage is an area of hitting that is extremely important and is overlooked by many hitters. The main goal in having plate coverage is to find the proper place in the batter's box for your hitting style and approach to the ball.

If the weight shift style is used, the general rule is deeper in the box and off the plate. Hitters using the rotation style generally should be at mid-point in the box and closer to the plate. Slight adjustments are O.K., because the way hitters approach the ball vary. Standing in the places described gives the barrel a chance to move consistently through the strike zone during the swing. Getting too far from the positions described goes against the principles of the two hitting styles. The weight shift style hitters who stands too close to the plate will get jammed if he strides properly. Rotation hitters who stand too far off the plate can lose plate coverage because of the outward rotation of their swing. The hit style the hitter uses and how they approach the ball, will be the deciding factor in where they stand in the box.

The hitters should be encouraged to experiment so they can find the right place in the batter's box every time. After finding the right place find a way to get there every time. Consistency is extremely important. If the hitter is not consistent, they will lack outside coverage one time then too much coverage the next.

One way to be consistent is using the bat as a measuring tool. You should step into a batter box and place your feet where you think they should be. After taking your normal stride and swing look at the barrel as it passes over the plate. Adjust the feet until you can see the barrel covering the plate. Once you have your feet where you want them touch a corner of the plate with the bat. This touch system assures you are in the same place each time you enter the box. Yankees great, Aaron Judge uses the touch system every time he gets into the batter's box.

There may be times when the hitter should move closer or farther from the plate. Game situations sometimes will dictate where the hitter stands. There will be times when the hitter would help the team by either pushing or pulling the ball. Don't be reluctant to make adjustments in the box that will help you carry out offensive strategy. (See chapter on offensive strategy.

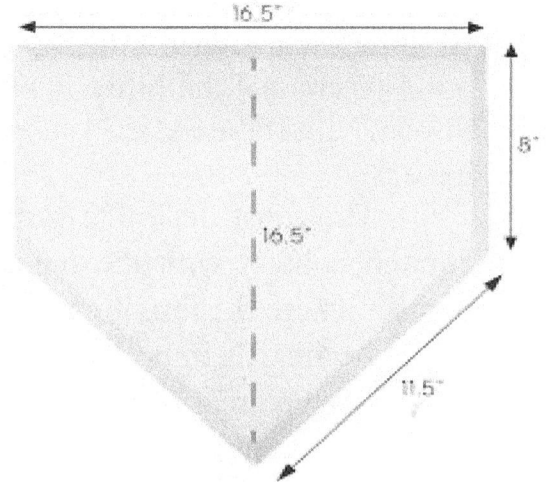

STRIKE ZONE DISCIPLINE
Ted Williams said it best : "My first rule of hitting was to get a good ball to hit"

It's very simple. Except for a very few gifted hitters, most find it much easier to hit if they hit strikes. I'm sure you have heard a pitching coach yell to his pitcher, "get ahead of the hitters". That tells you it must be easier for him to pitch when he's ahead. You must remember, if you swing at pitches three inches off the borders of the plate you have increased the strike zone over 30%. Swinging at pitches in this area, you will consistently hit behind in the count which is not to your advantage.

There are exceptions, but most of the great hitters in the game today are selective at the plate and work the pitchers into favorable counts. The question is how did they learn to select pitches? The most important thing, is knowing the importance of discipline at the plate. If you don't share this philosophy and its importance, you will never make an effort to work on the skills needed to judge balls and strikes.

Reading a pitch and making the decision to swing or not is a skill most hitters can learn through repetition. The hitters must make a conscious effort to make sure he/she is swinging at strikes in hitting practice. Also, a certain amount of batting practice must be at game like speed. You can do this by having the batting practice pitcher throw from a shorter distance. This cuts down the read time on the pitch making it appear to be at game like speed. From the shorter distance read the pitch and make the decision on whether to swing or not. By practicing this way, the hitter's quick judgement skills will improve greatly.

Hitting strikes is especially important with runners in scoring position. In these situations, the pitcher wants you to hit his pitch. Thus, he will miss more often, so the hitter must be patient and not get over anxious. This is extremely important if you expect to knock in the big runs.

Below is a study that was done in 1981 that proves the advantages of hitting ahead in the count. The following figures were compiled after 52 games and 1,741 at bats. They reflect the batting averages compiled with various counts.

0-0 .318	1-0 .359	2-0 .373	3-0 .250	1-1 .282	2-1 .366
3-1 .365	3-2 .263	0-1 .194	0-2 .094	1-2 .166	2-2 .263

Notice in every count, except 3-0 the hitter had a higher average when he was ahead in the count. Now you know why the pitching coach yells to his pitcher to pitch ahead! The game between the pitcher and hitter is a game within itself and the hitter can't beat himself if he's going to win that game. Ask any pitcher who they like to pitch to and most of them will say, the wild swinger.

We don't want a team full of nonaggressive hitters, but we do want hitters to understand the advantages of strike zone discipline. The thing to strive for, is **controlled aggression.**

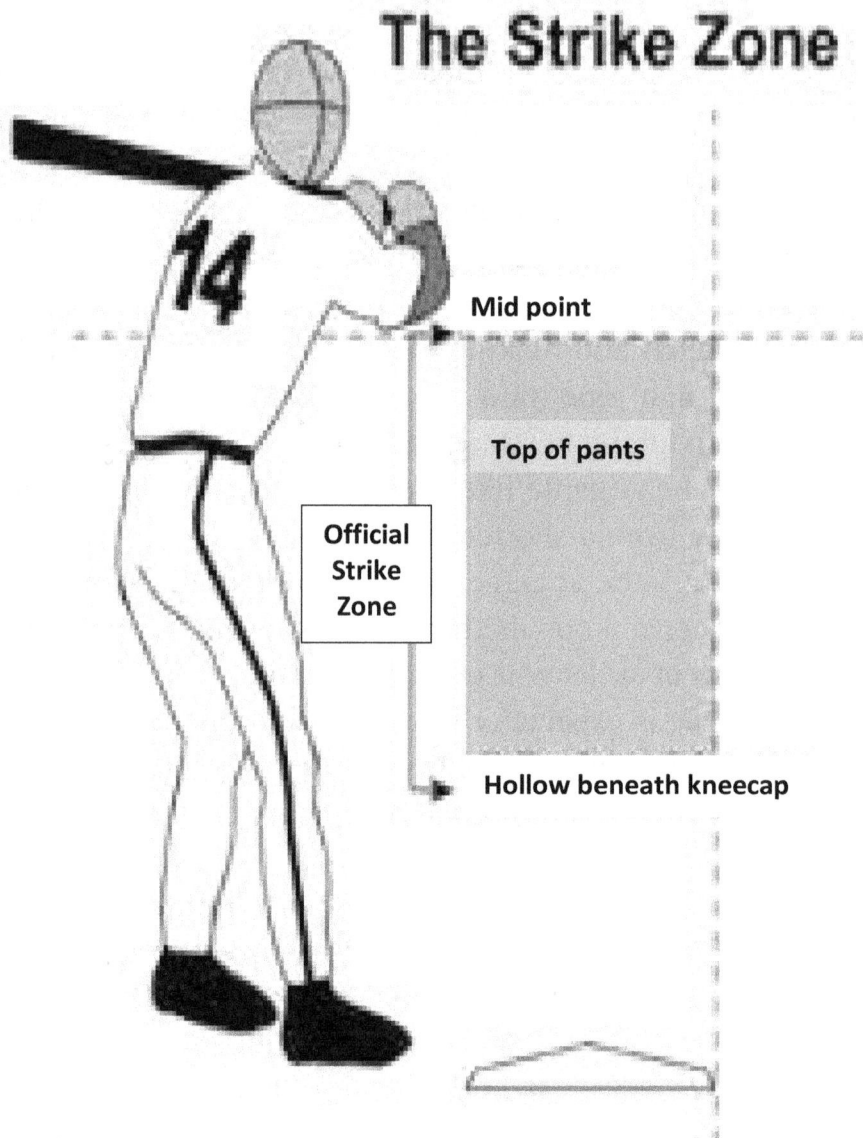

The Strike Zone

Mid point

Top of pants

Official
Strike
Zone

Hollow beneath kneecap

ULTIMATE INGREDIENTS FOR HITTING SUCCESS

a. **Desire** – *To wish, long for, or crave something.* Crave means: *to yearn for or desire intensely.*

You must be obsessed with your desire to hit. Hitting is a difficult skill to master. There are no short cuts, no easy ways out. There will be many bumps in the road, many tough moments. There will be series of bad at bats, bad games, bad weeks, and maybe even bad months. There may be thoughts of quitting or I can't hit. But if you start with a strong desire and you have the physical ability, you'll overcome any obstacle in your way. Every great Major League hitter has a burning desire to be the best he can be, and he won't let anything stand in his way.

b. **Patience** – *The capability of bearing delay.*

Every hitter wants positive results immediately. That's understandable, but that's not the way learning to hit works. Your journey is much like that of the baby learning to walk. The child first tries to get up then falls. It will get up, maybe take some steps. Then fall again, this process continues until he or she walks. Hitting is the same way. You'll have a bad day then make some adjustments and have some good days. Then you'll have some more bad days. The important thing is that you fully understand this is a process, there is no getting around it. The sooner you understand that this is a process that is unavoidable, the sooner you can stop beating up on yourself when you're struggling.

You have to realize that moving yourself from a sometimes-awkward young player into a pro prospect doesn't come over night. It takes day after day, month after month, season after season of perseverance and patience. So, concentrate on small steps, cementing them firmly into place one brick at a time. Soon you'll have a strong foundation to build on.

c **Faith**– *Believing in something which cannot be seen, heard, or proven.*

You must believe that through hard, smart work you'll be rewarded with success. You must believe that if you keep a positive attitude and learn something every day, you'll have a payoff. There will be times when you have no proof that you will succeed. You will have to believe. There will be times when you will lose faith in yourself. You must always go back and get it. Without faith you're going nowhere. Good things will always happen if you have faith. The word confidence is a key word that you'll need no matter what you do in life. It comes from two Latin words con – meaning with, and fides – meaning faith. "With faith" is confidence. Without faith there is zero confidence. That's how important faith is.

d **Dedication** – *To be devoted to a special purpose.*

You must want to become a better hitter and be dedicated to that purpose. You must set goals and let nothing stand in your way of reaching those goals. There will be lots of things trying to stop you – negative jealous people, drugs, laziness, curve balls, night life, bad days. But you must take a tough stand for what you want and not let anything get in your way. You should write the following statement down and read it every day.

"I WILL NEVER STOP WORKING TO GET BETTER, NO MATTER HOW HARD THE STRUGGLE MAY BE. I WILL PERSEVERE DESPITE THE HARD TIMES I HAVE AHEAD OF ME."

e. Confidence – *The thought of believing in something that has not already happened. The feeling of assurance or certainty.*

This is the toughest ingredient to acquire and keep. It comes and goes. The people who stay confident for longer periods have a positive light-hearted outlook. They have good attitudes and believe good things will happen. They forget bad days and never carry the negative past with them. They're always replacing a negative with a positive. It may be dinner, positive conversation with a special person, or a call home. Forgetting failures is the first step to regaining lost confidence. You can accomplish that by getting your mind on something else. It is also important to understand, that if you have patience, faith, and dedication, confidence will come.

f. Final Conscious Pre-swing Thought

Before discussing what, final conscious thought is, lets explain the difference between the conscious mind and the subconscious mind. The brain acts much like a computer in that it stores the information you put into it. The conscious or slow thinking mind is your inner voice. It's the voice with which you talk to yourself. The subconscious mind is the mind that allows you to react to a pitch and tells you how to swing.

The final pre-swing thought is the last thing you hear from your inner voice. It's your last thought before you react to the pitch. Since you can control this thought why not think positively? If your final thought is homerun, you're dead. It will cause you to tighten up and pull off the ball. If your mind is racing with negative thoughts your subconscious mind has difficulty taking over and performing the swing.

Your last conscious thought should be something individual since each hitter has different tendencies and different swing problems. If you have tight hands or shoulders your final thought might be, soft hands and let it happen or relax and feel the sweet spot. Whatever that thought is, trust it and make it a routine. It clears and relaxes the mind and allows the body to react naturally to the ball. At what time to use it is also an individual thing. As a general rule it is used just prior to when the pitcher releases the ball.

g. **Visual Reminders**

Hitting is said to be the single most difficult thing to do in sports. It will test your mind, body, and character. There will be good days and bad days. Even the best will fail 7 out of 10 times. To be an effective hitter it takes a lot of preparation. You also must learn to be your own coach. It takes learning what you have to do to be a consistent hitter. Preparing to hit is reminding yourself of basic principles and fundamentals.

Every hitter should compile a list of words or short phrases that will help clear the mind. Again, this list should be individualized so you can key your swing movement. This will help clear the mind of negative thoughts.

Some examples of visual reminders: relaxation, rhythm, and balance, stride slow & easy, keep hands back as I stride, head still, see the ball hit the bat, upper body stacked, level body parts, level swing plane, drive through the ball, quick hands, five hitting phases, stride slow & easy. Your list should contain words or phrases that cure your hitting problems. Before you compile your list, you have to analyze your hitting problems. You have to ask yourself, what do I do wrong when I'm not swinging the bat well? These words or phrases should be written down on a piece of paper and looked at when needed. You'd be surprised how it can explain a bad day at the plate and give you something to work on the next day.

h. **The Level Cut. Line Drive Swing.**

Kids start playing organized tee ball at age 5 & 6 years old and normally use bats too heavy for their underdeveloped arms and hands. So, they drop their back shoulder and swing with their big muscles in a long sweeping action. This drops the bat barrel behind the body in a long arc and causes the hitter to lift the ball off the tee rather than drive through the ball. Another thing that programs the long upper cut is the thrill of the touchdown pass, the slam dunk, and the home run. We see them every night on a Sport Center, Griffey, Thomas, Bonds, Judge, and all the rest of them hitting 400-foot homeruns. The hard ground ball line-drive swing is what you should strive for. Why? Because 90% of fly balls are unproductive, while only 60% of ground balls are. A team that hits 27-line drives or ground balls will score a few runs in the 7th inning while a team that hits 27 fly balls will have a difficult time scoring runs.

BASIC HITTING PHILOSOPHY

Swing mechanics – Mastery of the basic swing mechanics.
Concentration – The ability to become absorbed in the action of hitting.
Confidence – The deep belief you can hit any pitcher.
Strike zone discipline – The ability to judge balls and strikes.

SWING MECHANICS

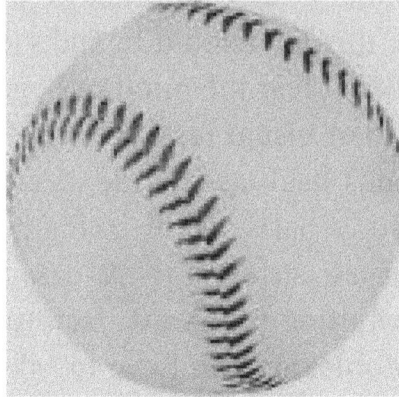

CONCENTRATION   **STRIKE ZONE DISCIPLINE**

CONFIDENCE

Each one of these four things feed off each other making the other possible. It starts with the basic mechanics of the swing. If you have mastered them you will get base hits. If you get base hits your confidence level will increase. With a high level of confidence, you will be able to relax and concentrate. With a high level of concentration, you will see the ball better, enabling you to judge balls and strikes. As you can see, you can't have one without the other, and without all four, it is difficult to become a complete hitter.

There are three basic goals every hitter should have whenever he/she picks up a baseball bat:
   Direction – Learn to control the bat so you can control the ball. In batting practice learn to hit holes and the gaps.
   Height – Hit the ball at the proper height, which is on the line. Homeruns will come.
   Velocity – Hit the ball hard so it will find the holes and the gaps.

BASIC OFFENSIVE STRATEGY

To understand the offensive part of the game of baseball, one must realize that the offensive part is no different than any other team sport. That is, each hitter has his/her responsibility according to the play being run, the situation of the game, or the count they are hitting in during the inning.

Just like the running back in football, his responsibilities change from play to play according to the situation of the game. Because hitting is an individual skill, one sometimes forgets about offensive strategy and situation hitting.

What you will read on the following is nothing complicated. They are basic things every player must know and understand before the team can succeed. The objective in this section is to get hitters to realize the importance of executing basic offensive strategy. If you don't know the importance of offensive strategy, you won't work on the skills needed to make that strategy work.

Every player must know there is more to hitting than just swinging the bat. Every player should realize they are given the chance to execute offensive strategy by the manager for the good of the team. Every hitter on the team is part of an offensive unit. That unit is nine hitters against one pitcher. Just think about that. How can one pitcher beat nine hitters if they are working together?

The following are three basic goals every team should have:
1. Getting runners on base. (Preferably the leadoff hitter of the inning.)
2. Advancing the runner or runners.
3. Scoring the runner or runners.

Every player must realize if the team is going to be successful offensively, each hitter has a role or job. The hitter also must realize that the job changes with each at bat, according to the situation of the game. The hitter, before the start of the inning, must know what the team needs to win the game and how his job will change as the inning progresses.

It is the hitter's responsibility at the start of an inning to know the following:
1. The score of the game.
2. What inning it is.
3. How many outs there are as the inning progresses.

Going over these things in our mind beforehand, will make it easier for the hitter to respond to the manager's strategy as the inning unfolds. Also, if you know the manager's strategy ahead of time, it will be easier to perform the skills needed to execute the strategy. Don't ever be caught by surprise. Being surprised is being unprepared and failure is a by-product of not being prepared.

HITTING PHILOSOPHIES & THEORIES

Because players vary in physical characteristics', hitting style must also vary. There are three basic hitting styles. Identify what style is suited for the player than perfect the fundamentals of that style.

Every hitter must develop a hitting style to take advantage of their physical characteristics. A player's physical characteristics, his running speed, strength, hand-quickness, physical size and eye-hand coordination vary. It is important for both players and coaches to understand this principle. No two players are alike. Each have different body types, bone length and muscle structure, etc. But they do fit into certain categories.

Some have great speed, others average speed. Some have great strength while some have average strength. Some have great bat quickness and others have average bat quickness. All hitters are not created equal. So, you can't make them into something they can't become. Once this principle is understood; each player can fit into one of the basic hitting styles. Only then can a player reach his/her full offensive potential.

<u>**Example:**</u> Not every hitter can hold their hands close to their body, bat vertical, use the top hand and be quick like Ted Williams. But they may be able to hold their hands back, flatten their bat, pull with the bottom hand and shift their weight like George Brett.

The movements of each hitting style differ and each hitter has control over the style he/she decides to use. Just like the doctor, coaches can give hitters a prescription to develop their hitting style. Through repetition, one can acquire and make the movements of that style become natural. The key to perfecting hitting movements is working slowly and deliberately. It is a progression process from dry swings, to tee swings, to batting practice, and finally to the game.

It's important to remember each movement must be consciously thought about and practiced in order to make it part of your muscle memory. Muscle memory is identical to mind memory. Read a paragraph 5 times and you won't have it memorized. Read if five more times and you'll remember a few phrases and maybe a few sentences. Read it 100 time aloud and you will have it memorized. Muscle memory works the same way. Perform the movements of hitting over and over correctly and you can't help developing a sound swing. If you are practicing the movements incorrectly you will put the incorrect movements into your muscle memory. So, it is always important to have a coach monitor your progress.

Many people say great hitters are born not made. This is not totally true. Don't misunderstand this statement; there were many great natural born hitters. Rod Carew, Tony Oliva, Ted Williams, Stan Musial, Al Kaline, Derek Jeter, and Ty Cobb, to name a few, were all real natural hitters. But for every natural born hitter there are five who made themselves great hitters by having good work habits such as George Brett. Pete Rose, Carl Yastrezski, Wade Boggs, Hal McRea, Lou Piniella, Dewy Evans, Kirby Puckett, Matt Williams, and one of the best examples is Mike Schmidt. Each one of these guys had to work extra hard to perfect their hitting styles. But more importantly, these hitters had to work smart to reach the level they did. They had to get in the batting cage and really use their heads to make themselves become great. Remember, great athletes learn their skills then compete with their minds. The smarter man will ultimately win the day.

Notes:

MENTAL SKILLS FOR HITTERS

The mental side of hitting is extremely critical. Having a <u>positive</u> mental attitude every game, every at bat, and every pitch over the long baseball season is the most important asset a hitter can possess. Without it, the hitter can't concentrate and control their nervous system to allow their hitting skills to work. Without it, the hitter can't concentrate and control their nervous system to allow his/her hitting skills to work.

Do you know the difference between a .270 hitter and a .310 hitter each with 500 at bat (AB's)? The difference is only one hit a week over the 20-week minor league season. Just think of that, only one hit a week separates the average hitter from the best hitters. How many AB's have you given away because you were not ready mentally to hit? How many because of lack of intensity, lack of concentration, lack of determination, thinking of past performances, self-doubt, pressing and trying too hard, not relaxing, thinking too much, being negative? These mental distractions make hitters do the things they do at the plate. They cause the mechanical problems. **Change the way you think, and you can change the way you hit.**

The confrontation between the pitcher and hitter is a game within a game. It's very challenging and it will test the hitter's character. This game is either won or lost by what goes on between the hitter's ears. It is just as important to learn mental skills as it is to learn the physical skills of hitting. There have been hitters with good mechanics but a bad mental attitude who didn't hit.

The biggest obstacle a hitter has, is a negative mind set. Their mind sometimes can be their biggest handicap. It can also be their biggest asset. Being a successful hitter depends more on strength of mind than strength of body. When the hitter starts to understand what goes on inside of them, they will be able to manage themself and their attitude.

Important points:
1. The difference between a .270 hitter and a .310 hitter is one hit a week. Learn why you did or didn't get that hit! If you didn't make it, it may be your attitude.
2. The game between the pitcher and hitter is won or lost by what goes on between your ears.
3. Your mind can be either your greatest handicap or your greatest asset.

There are mental skills the player can learn so they can manage, their mental state. These skills are important as they allow them to have a consistent, more positive frame of mind. They also will help control the nervous system so the hitter can relax. When the are relaxed and focused, their hitting skills are free to react to the pitch.

Learning to deal with all the distractions and mind games is essential if the hitter are going to reach their full potential. The high-performance state of mind leads to high concentration level, composure under pressure, clear vision, and mental strategy that leads to peak performance. This is the mind set of all great athletes. This separates great hitters from average hitters. The great hitters train their minds just as hard as they train their swing mechanics. Great hitters develop mental fitness.

To the player:

When you develop and use mental fitness skills, you create a state of relaxed concentration. You are relaxed physically, in control of your thinking, feeling positive, confident, and you have a sense of just letting it happen at the plate.

Most athletes have little training in mental skills; therefore, they don't know the importance of learning those skills. It is important to understand it's no different than learning any other skill.

How many times have you heard the hitter say, "I'm not seeing the ball" or "I don't feel good at the plate?" Not being able to see the ball or not feeling good are mental problems which in turn become physical problems. When you go to the plate with self-doubt your nervous system gets out of whack. This causes muscle tension, which "pinches" nerve impulses. This results in the tightening of the muscles in your eyes, hands, and legs. This is why you don't see the ball or feel good. You are tight, anxious, and jumpy, instead of relaxed and smooth.

Important points:
1. Mental fitness leads to a peak performance state of mind. This leads to high levels of concentration, clear vision, composure under pressure and mental strategy.
2. Great athletes train their minds just as hard as their bodies.
3. Self-doubt causes muscle tension which leads to bad vision, tight hands and legs.

Learning mental skills to help stay in a positive mental state starts with taking a mental inventory. You must be aware of what you're feeling mentally when you are going good and what you're feeling mentally when you are going bad. Your mental state will change from day to day and you must be aware of where you are at the present time. Once you are aware, you can change and control how you think and feel. If you can mentally review each pitch of your at bats and remember how you felt; you're on the way to developing mental fitness.

Only after sensing what's going on inside of you, as a result of several bad at bats, can you begin to do something about how you feel. Until you can control the way you think and feel you will be fighting an uphill battle.

It starts with sensing how you feel and what you're thinking in certain situations during the game. You must ask yourself, and be honest, how did I really feel. What was I thinking before, during, and after each at bat? Was I a little nervous? If I was, did my hands tighten up? Was I really focused and feeling confident? Was I intense and determined to succeed? Was I intimidated in any way? Did I really want to be up with the game on the line? How you think and feel during an at bat will have a direct effect on your pitch selection and how you swing the bat. This is taking **mental inventory.**

You can't separate how you are thinking and feeling from how your body is working. The mind and body are directly connected. The professional hitter understands their mind can get out of focus and knows what to do about it. They simply talk themself back to where they want their mind to be and feeds their mind positive self-talk. They don't allow negative thought processes to occupy their mind; They clear it out before entering the batter's box. This is why the professional hitter appears relaxed and confident at the plate. They can sense when their mind is wandering or if they feel tight. But more importantly, they can get their mind back on track by using mental fitness skills.

Be aware of three things when taking mental inventory; the physical body, your feelings, and your mind. Messages from the physical body include sweaty palms, increased heart rate, red face, shaking legs, tight hands. Messages from feelings are anger, fear, calmness, helplessness, depression, and frustration. Messages from the mind would be lack of focus, negative thoughts, not staying in the now, and doubt. This is taking mental inventory; observing this information is the first step to mental fitness.

Important Points:
1. Taking inventory is the start of changing what's going on inside of you.
2. Change the way you think and feel and you're on your way to becoming a seasoned hitter.
3. The mind and body are closely connected. Control the mind and you'll control the body.
4. The professional hitter uses positive self-talk to get focused; this allows them to master the body.
5. You must recognize messages you are receiving from your body, your feelings, and your mind.

When taking inventory, you must develop active awareness. Active awareness simply means being alert to how you are feeling at any given time.

a. Active awareness has three steps:
1. Step back, slow down, and observe what's going on inside of you. This first step clears the mind and allows you to be creative.

2. Make a choice and decide what you need for your body to work as you want.

3. Act, do something to adjust or correct what's going on inside you.

An example would be this: sometimes before or during an at bat you may feel lethargic. Being aware of this you can pump yourself up. Other times you will need to gear yourself down as you maybe too excited. The important thing is, to observe how you feel, choose what you need to do, and act on those decisions.

This process of observe, choose, and act doesn't only apply to the physical it applies to what's going on in your mind. If you observe that you're out of focus or tight, you must change this before you hit. If you are doubting yourself, you must use positive self-talk before you get in the box. Until you become aware of how you feel and what's going on in your head, you'll never reach your full potential. When you start to understand and put into practice the observe, choose, and act principle, you are on your way to becoming a seasoned hitter. If you do not, you may become your most potent adversary.

To change and control how you feel you will need to learn and perfect the following skills:

1. **Optimism** – The ability to think positively at difficult challenging times.
2. **Imagery** – The ability to see yourself succeeding.
3. **Energy management** – Not getting too high or too low.
4. **Vision** – Being able to see yourself succeeding in the future.
5. **Attention skills** – The ability to focus.
6. **Mental preparation** – Being ready mentally by using positive self-talk.

Optimism is looking for an opportunity in difficult, challenging situations. One such situation might go like this: It's the bottom of the ninth, score tied. The best pitcher in the league is on the mound. The opportunities are, you have a chance to put your ability against his and a chance to win the game. You must tell yourself this is competition at its best, this is exciting, this is where you want to be. You have trained your swing and body for this moment. Why throw all that work down the drain with anything but an optimistic mind set?

A positive mental attitude is the most powerful asset a hitter possesses. The baseball season is a long grueling grind. The hitter who has the ability to forget bad performances is well on his way to becoming an optimistic person.

Here is an example of how an optimistic person and a pessimistic person might view the same situation. The situation is this: you have had three bad games and the third ends with a strike-out. You are now 0 for your last 12. The pessimistic person might talk in statements like this.

"Boy I've lost it. I can't hit anymore. That first pitch of my third AB was right there, how could I miss it. Another couple of bad days and I'll be 0-20 and on the bench.

The optimistic person might think like this: "I've had a couple of bad days but even the best hitters have them. I remember George Brett took an 0-25 once. It's a long season. I've got to realize I'm not going to hit well all the time. The important thing is to keep a good positive attitude. Tomorrow I'll make some adjustments and get back on track."

The optimistic person perceives their problem as a challenge, something they can correct. They also see the problem as a way to increase their knowledge of hitting. They learn from their mistakes and know they will make them better in the long term. The player who approaches a bad game or series of bad games with the proper attitude gives themselves a better chance to succeed the next day. <u>Remember, you are always preparing for the future</u>. The past is over; you can't bring it back.

Those of us not blessed with an optimistic attitude can learn it. But before we take the time to learn it, we must understand its importance and benefits. You must realize all great accomplishments, whether in the business world or on the athletic field, are done by positive, optimistic people. Once you understand how important it is to be optimistic, you are ready to learn an important new skill. The skill is called, *reframing*.

Important Points:
1. Active awareness has three steps: observe, choose, and act. Until you learn this principle you will be a prisoner to your mind.
2. We use active awareness to inventory how we feel.
3. To change and control our attitude we must learn the following: Optimism, imagery, energy management, vision, attention skills, and mental preparation.

b. Reframing: *Get yourself in a positive frame of mind.*

Reframing is taking any situation, especially a negative one, and choosing to focus on the opportunity of that situation. The frame in the word reframing is the perception we bring to the situation. We can't often control events that are happening to us, but we can change the way we see those events.

One situation might be: you are in a terrible slump; it is the ninth inning and the winning run is on second. Where is the opportunity in this situation? That is the question we ask ourselves in order to reframe. Naturally you would rather be going to the plate coming off a 4-4 streak, but you are not. So, if you want to have a quality at bat and have a chance to drive in that run, you better focus on the opportunity. If you focus on the fact that you are not feeling good, your chances of succeeding go way down. You have got to pump yourself up, get very determined.

It is not easy to perceive opportunity in tough situations. It takes a level head, imagination, creativity, and character to think positive at difficult times. The opportunity in the above situation may be to learn to relax and face a tough situation head on and have a quality at bat. Learn to believe in yourself, even if you are having a tough time. Learn to develop character for similar situations in the future. Choosing to focus on positive thoughts and feelings allows your body to relax and perform.

One of the most common ways of sabotaging an at bat is talking to yourself in negative ways. Sometimes this happens when you are in a bad streak. Either before you go to the plate or in between pitches your self-talk should be what you want, not what you don't want. Your thinking must be, "I want to get a hit or I want to hit the ball hard." If you think it, believe it, you are halfway there. If you don't, you are leaving your at bat to chance.

When you are going well, the process of positive self-talk and confidence building happens naturally. But when you are struggling, it is very important for you to constantly be aware what is going on in your mind. If your mind is racing with negative thoughts, you have to change them before you hit. Don't let your mind control you. Control your mind.

Positive self-talk starts in the dugout. It starts with observing the pitcher and developing your plan. What type of movement does his/her breaking ball and his/her fast ball have? Is he/she/ throwing both pitches for strikes? If he/she is not, what is their location? Where is his/her release point? Watch the action of hitters ahead of you. This type of preparation is positive. It is the first step to getting your mind together.

Pete Rose had a habit. After he made an out, he would sit on the top step of the dugout, rather than the bench. He did this a number of times. When asked why he did this, He said, "Being alone and getting my mind back on the game helps me forget my last at bat." The key word here is to forget. Getting his mind back on the game helped Pete forget the out he just made. His mind was occupied by the game; thus, it was impossible for the negative process to happen. It is very important to understand, the moments he started observing the game his negative thoughts were gone. The ending of his negative thoughts, if he had them, began the positive self-talk process.

Another way to stop negative thinking is to talk to a friend or teammate about something other than baseball. There are many other ways to end the negative thought process. What ways can you think of?

Once you have cleared the mind of negative thoughts you are now able to feed yourself short positive phrases to give you a positive mind set. Some of these phrases could be:

1. I can hit this guy.
2. I am better than him.
3. Today is my day. I know I am going to get a hit.
4. This guy is mine.
5. I am going to look for his fast ball and whack it.

6. This guy is not going to get me out.
7. I am relaxed, confident, and in control.

Feeling determined is another way to erase negative thoughts. Being determined puts you on the offense. It will pump you up and give you positive energy.

Remember, what you say to yourself will directly affect how you feel. Thinking negatively will get you feeling bad and thinking positively will make you feel good. Don't you feel good when someone tells you how good you are? Hearing it from yourself has the same effect, if you do it enough. A good example of this is Mohammed Ali, "I am the greatest." He used to say this all the time. Every time he said it, he reinforced his confidence in himself. Every time he made that statement, that positive thought was ingrained deeper and deeper in his mind. There is no doubt Ali had tremendous physical talents, but the strongest part of his body was his mind.

You do not have to go around telling everyone how great you are, but a little positive self-talk sure helps your attitude. The greatest thing about the power of positive thinking, is the mind does not know the difference between something imagined and something that is real. The point is, imagining being successful has the same effect on the mind as if it really happened. To put it simply, the mind absorbs and stores what you tell it. It also absorbs and stores what it hears from other people. Learn to talk to yourself in a positive way and surround yourself with positive people. If you do you will be on your way to controlling events affecting your life.

Important Points:
1. Reframing is the skill of learning to see opportunity in difficult times and challenging situations.
2. Be your own best friend, learn to talk to yourself in a positive way.
3. Feeling determined puts you on the offensive and erases negative thoughts.
4. The mind does not know the difference between something that has really happened and something that is imagined.
5. Observation can stop negative thinking and clear the mind.
6. Feed your mind positive one-line phrases to instill confidence.

**Reframing can be used in any sport or anywhere
you need to get yourself into a positive frame of mind.**

Running a Good Practice

It is easier to be prepared for practice if you have developed a good instructional plan. It is important that the players work on less difficult goals in early season practice. As your players master basic skills you then can begin to introduce more advanced skills. One new objective should be established for each practice with a number of activities and drills used to teach the new skill.

Your practices should be run under a basic format that includes:

- **Warm up** – to warm up the muscles to reduce risk of injuries.
- **Practice previously taught skills** – To work on fundamental skills already learned.
- **Teach and practice new skills** – To build on player's existing skills.
- **Practice under game-like conditions** – To stimulate competition.
- **Cool down** – To allow athlete's bodies to return to resting state and avoid stiffness.
- **Evaluate** – To discuss with your players if objectives were achieved during practice.

All players should have an equal chance to participate and always match player's ability and physical maturity. If you break your team into groups make sure all groups are matched as equally as possible to avoid one group from always winning. Never put pressure on always winning but emphasize performing well while giving each player room to make mistakes. Your players will have more fun if they know they will be rewarded if they work hard and are praised when they do well.

Practice Drills

Drills are a great way to review old skills, work on new ones, and even simulate game conditions. The following drills are just a few examples. There are many more. Incorporate them into your practice and always be on the lookout for more. Choose the ones that work on basic skills for earlier practices, then proceed to specialized drills as the first game approaches.

Throwing – To help strengthen throwing muscles and learn throwing accuracy.

Pair up players with each pair having a baseball to throw to each other. Have the catcher give a target with the glove and the thrower throw to the glove. Alternate catcher and thrower with each throw. To create competition, give the thrower one point if the ball would have hit the catcher's body and two points for the head. The first to score 21 points wins.

Coaching Points – Encourage the thrower to concentrate at throwing to the glove. Make sure the throwers are throwing over the top, not side-arm.

Grounders – To practice the fundamentals of fielding ground balls and quick ball release.

Break players into two lines. Position one line at the shortstop position, and the other line at second base position. Have a player start at first base. Hit a ground ball to the first in line at shortstop. After the players at shortstop catch the grounder and throws to first, he rotates to the end of the line at second base. The player at second base moves to first base after making the play. The player at first base rotates to the end of the line at shortstop after catching throws from both lines. Increase the speed of the game as fielding improves.

Coaching Points – Make sure each player is fielding the grounder correctly and using two hands for quick ball release. This drill is good for working on previously taught skills.

Notes:

_____
_____
_____
_____
_____
_____
_____
_____
_____
_____
_____
_____
_____
_____
_____
_____
_____
_____
_____
_____
_____
_____
_____

Batting Practice Routine

Batting practice routine should be used to simulate, as much as possible, game situations. This can involve both the hitter and fielders. It is easy for young and even older players to lose focus if not involved or active. Baseball is a game where the action can sometimes be slow. It is important to develop a well-organized practice where players are not just standing around. The following batting practice routines are designed to help coaches work on individual problems, develop strike zone discipline, stimulate competition, and teach team unity while keeping all players focused.

There are many ways to set up a batting practice routine but try to develop an easy routine at the beginning then progress to more complex routines as the players improve and mature. One thing that can be guaranteed with a controlled, organized and well-run routine is that each player can and will improve.

Control must be established at the first practice. Never let the players start the practice with hitting or without an order how batters will hit. Batting order is a way to establish hitting order. Another is the order the players arrive at practice. This is good since it encourages players to get to practice early or on time.

A good way to warm-up hitting muscles is to have the on-deck hitter hit off a tee into the backstop. By starting off with the tee, coaches have a perfect opportunity to use the drills in this manual to work on individual problems.

Never go into hitting practice without a set routine on how many swings each batter takes. Any more then fifteen (15) swings at one time is too many. It is better to go five (5) to ten (10) swings two or three times instead of allowing the hitter to continue to hit over and over. This is how bad habits are formed.

Each hitter should bunt the first three (3) to five (5) pitches so that he/she can learn to bunt. This also helps the batter follow the ball to the bat and get used to the speed of the pitch. The bunts should be towards the first or third base line.

Drill: A good way to work on bunting and stimulate competition is to have all the players line up at home plate to bunt. The object is to be the last player in the game. To continue to play, the ball must be bunted fair. If foul, the batter is out of the game. Losers must run a lap around the bases.

Coaching Points - Check to make sure all the hitters are bunting correctly. If any are having a problem, take them aside to work with them. Do this drill only two (2) or three (3) times. It moves pretty quickly, and it is fun for the kids.

Another good way to promote competition is to set-up two- or three-man hitting teams. Try to match each team as equally as possible so that each has a chance to win. Fielders are set-up in normal fielding positions. The object for the hitters is to get base hits. And the object of the fielders is to get three outs.

Each hitter steps into the box as if it were a game. Balls and strikes are called but no walks are allowed since this is hitting practice. Errors are not counted as hits and the fielders must throw out the runners or catch fly balls to make outs. Just like a game. Since hits are counted and there is a winner and loser, all players stay focused and work really hard to get hits or make outs. It is as close to game conditions as possible without playing a game. It is important that the manager or coach maintain control of calling balls and strikes and determining errors and hits by controlling calls, discipline and control can be and must be established. A team that has managers and coaches in control has a better chance of improving and winning games.

Notes:

_____
_____
_____
_____
_____
_____
_____
_____
_____
_____
_____
_____
_____
_____
_____
_____
_____
_____
_____
_____
_____
_____
_____
_____
_____
_____
_____

Advanced Batting Practice Routine

The main goals of this format are:

1. To develop practice habits that allow hitters to take advantage of their abilities.
2. To perfect the skills necessary to produce a line drive swing with maximum bat speed and aggressiveness.
3. For hitters to perfect the skills of situation hitting.

First Round

Two (2) Sacrifice Bunts.

One (1) Squeeze Bunt.

One (1) Fake Bunt & Slash.

Four (4) Situation Swings A, B, C, D (Determined each day)

    A. Hit and Run.

    B. Move runner from 2nd to 3rd no outs.

    C. Get runner in from 3rd infield back.

    D. Get runner in from 3rd infield in.

Four (4) Swings: The hitter's mind set is being above the ball and on top. His/her mind set is to hit the ball towards the opposite side of the mound on the ground.

One (1) Bunt for a base hit (run to first base and become a runner.)

Second Round

Four (4) Swings: The hitter's mind set is to hit the ball on a line to the gaps. Aggressiveness and bat speed are increased.

Third Round

Number of swings are determined by the manager and swings are used to make adjustment from earlier rounds.

All pre-game practice is for the purpose of hitting line drives. Hitters are not attempting to lift the ball over the fence. Poor batting practice creates bad habits which consequently result in poor game performance. All work on mechanics and individual instruction should be done during extra batting practice.

SITUATION HITTING

PROPER EXECUTION IN SITUATIONS RESULTS IN WINNING BASEBALL.

KNOW THE SITUATION YOU ARE IN AND WHAT YOU HAVE TO DO TO ADVANCE BASE RUNNERS.
KNOW THE PITCHER AND WHAT HE/SHE WILL PROBABLY DO TO TRY TO GET AN OUT.
USE BATTING PRACTICE ROUTINE TO PRACTICE EXECUTION OF SITUATION HITTING.

The following are hitting situations that are important to the team in building consistent scoring attack. Also, these situations are flexible according to the manager's philosophy. The manager will let the hitter know what his/her role is when it comes to situation hitting. Not every hitter will be asked to carry out every one of the following situations. Every hitter should know the purpose of situation hitting and how it fits into the manager's offensive strategy.

1. **Lead-Off hitter In the Game**
   The hitter should take a strike if the count goes to 2-0. Some starting pitchers struggle early in the game with their control. Getting the starter in trouble early is important so make them prove they can throw strikes.
2. **Hitter Leading Off an Inning When A New Pitcher Enters**
   The hitter takes 2-0 late in the game, depending on the game situation and manager's preference. The exception here is if the hitter can zone for their pitch. By zoning their chances for the extra base hit that would put the winning run in scoring position are greater. A relief pitcher can struggle when he/she enters the game. Make sure they can throw strikes and always let them beat themselves.
3. **Runner Held at First**
   Left-handed Hitter – When the runner is held at first early in the count, the hitter should look to pull the ball in the hole between first and second.
   Right-Handed Hitter – When the runner is held at first, the hitter should look for a ball to drive in the hole between first and second.

Runner Stealing Base – The hitter should zone for their pitch and swing if it is in their personal hitting zone, but take if it is not. The exception here is if the game is close late in the game. The hitter may want to take, to allow the base stealer to get into scoring position.

Hitting to the hole between first and second is an important skill to execute for a few reasons.

One, by hitting the ball in the hole to right field the runner on first can advance more than one base. Each ninety (90) feet is one-fourth of a run and the closer the runner is to home plate the easier it is to produce a full run. Also, the team is only going to get so many hits in each game, so the hitter must move each runner as many bases as possible with each hit.

Second, by attempting to hit the hole it is easier to stay out of the double play when the ball is hit to the right side.

Third, if a fast runner is on first and the hitter doesn't succeed in hitting the ball through the hole. He forces the second baseman to go to first. Looking for and reacting to the right pitch, plus moving up or back from the plate are keys to executing the skills mentioned, to hitting to the right side.

4. **Runner on Second No Outs – Early in the Game**

   Left-handed Hitter – Should attempt to drive the runner in by pulling the ball to right field. The hitter may move closer to the plate to get a pitch to pull.

   Right-handed Hitter – Should attempt to drive the run in by hitting ball to the right side. The hitter may move off the plate in order for the ball to be out over the plate.

   Early in the game the hitter is not giving themselves up. At this point in the game, you are looking for the big inning and you do not want to give up outs. In the attempt to drive the ball to the right side and if the hitter does not get a hit, the runner still moves up to third base.

   Two exceptions would be, if the hitter is not swinging the bat well, or you are facing a pitcher with which you have had trouble. In both cases the hitter may want to give themselves up to move the runner.

5. **Runner on Second with No Outs Late in The Game (Score Close)**

   Left-handed Hitter – Must make contact and pull the ball to the right side.

   Right-handed Hitter – Must make contact and hit the ball to the right side.

   In both cases the hitter's mind set should be, keep the ball out of the air and getting the runner over to third. The hitter may choke up on the bat for more control and they should always choke up with two strikes. Here you are playing for the run to win the game and you are willing to give up an out to get that run.

6. **Runner on Third Less Than Two Outs (infield up)**

   The hitter's mind set is to drive the ball on a line to the center fielder, but it does not mean he must hit it there. This mind set helps the hitter stay on the ball. The hitter must keep the ball away from the corners. Some pitchers will throw a change up or curve in this situation hoping for the ground ball to the corners. The hitter should not try to lift the ball in this situation and their mind set is a line drive stroke.

7. **The runner on Third Less Than Two Outs (infield back)**

    The hitter's mind set is to drive the ball to center fielder until they has one strike. After the hitter has one strike they should chokes up, shortens their swing, gets on top of the pitch, and hits the ball up the middle away from the corners.

8. **Hit and Run**

    Runner at first breaks and the hitter protects the runner. Hitter's number one job is to make contact and their number two responsibility is to hit the ball on the ground. The hitter should hit the ball where it is pitched, since hitting to the vacated hole can be difficult on certain pitches. Think, stay on top of the ball.

9. **Butting situations**

    Runner on first base - Make the first basemen field the bunt.

    Runner on first and second – Make the worst fielder (first or third basemen) field the bunt. It is safer to kill the ball toward first base than it is to try to bunt it past the pitcher to the third baseman. The exception would be if the first baseman is an excellent fielder who can throw the runner out at third base.

    Make the pitcher throw a strike. A walk is better than a sacrifice bunt. Also, if the hitter can get an advantage in the count the manager knows he can bunt with one strike. The hitter should know when the situation calls for a drag bunt or push ball for a hit. If the hitter becomes a good bunter the manager may give him/her bunt for a hit sign.

10. **Bunting for a Base Hit**

    This is a weapon that all hitters should be able to use, especially faster runners. The reputation of being able to bunt for a hit will bring the infielders in and create more holes for ground ball hits. Practicing bunting techniques will give you confidence to bunt for a hit and not feel it is a wasted at bat. Know when the situation is good to bunt. The following are not good situations to try to bunt for a hit.

    a. Two outs, no one on, and the hitter is not a base stealer or they have the ability to hit a double.

    b. Two outs runner on second base. A bunt won't score the run.

    c. Ahead by a lot of runs.

    d. Late in the game and the hitter has extra base power.

11. **Fake bunt and slash**

Whenever the sacrifice bunt is on, in a first and second situation, the hitter has the option to fake a bunt and slash if the infielders are moving in. Watch for the wheel play by the opposing manager in the first and second situation late in the game.

Proper execution of the slash is to turn to bunt with weight on the hitter's back foot. The bat is pulled back and the ball is slapped on the ground past the charging infielders.

Notes:

_____

_____

_____

_____

_____

_____

_____

_____

_____

_____

_____

_____

_____

_____

_____

_____

_____

_____

_____

_____

_____

_____

_____

_____

_____

Off-season Training

Off-Season is the time to work on increasing strength, endurance, and develop mental capabilities: a perfect time to work on basic skills, concentration, and develop good work habit. It is a time to work on weaknesses and allow injuries to heal.

Training should include weight training for the major muscle groups, sprints for quickness, and long distance running for cardiovascular development. For the young athlete, light weight with high reps is recommended and a maximum of two sets. The weight training should be done at least twice a week. Endurance training should be performed three times a week. This could include running, cross-country skiing, cycling, or anything to make the heart work harder for at least twenty minutes.

Remember, any additional strength will improve performance. Also, do not expect the youngster to automatically develop good work habits. It is up to you the parent, coach, grandparent, friend, or whoever to find time and a positive way to encourage the development of an off-season training program. Make the off-season training fun and take the time to make training a way of life. Both you and the ball player will become better friends.

Off-season training should also include hitting off the tee. This allows the hitter to work on the fundamentals of the swing while strengthening the hitting muscles. This can be done anywhere in the cellar, garage, or anywhere you can hang a hitting screen, net, or blanket. This also can be done inside when it is too cold outside. The hitter should swing a heavier bat to warm up and cool down. This will help strengthen the hitting muscles.

Notes:

_____

_____

_____

_____

_____

_____

_____

_____

_____

_____

_____

HITTING DRILLS

This is a pencil drawing of Steve when he played in Little League.
By Rich Braun, Steve's brother.

The movement of each hitting style and each hitter has control over the style they decides to use. Just like a doctor, coaches can give hitters a prescription to develop their hitting style. Through repetition, one can acquire and make the movements of that style become natural. The key is **conscious methodical repetition**, not just going to the cage or hitting off a tee and beating baseballs without a purpose. The key to perfecting hitting movements is working *slowly and deliberately*. It is a progression from dry swings, to tee swings, to batting practice, and finally to the game.

DRILLS

Problem: Poor Balance in Stance

Drill 1 Jump up and land

Player gets into his/her stance and jump vertically while maintaining his/her stance. When he/she reaches the ground he/she should feel connected to the ground with a solid leg base.

Drill 2 Push over

Attempt to push over the player from all angles, front, back, and both sides. Try to surprise him/her with your push. This will check his/her stability. If he/she has stability and balance, emphasizes that he/she is connected to the ground with their feet.

Drill 3 Blind swing

Take a dry swing with eyes closed. Hitter should focus on his/her feet and legs. He/she should have a feeling of stability and a solid connection to the ground.

Problem: Stepping In the Bucket And Front Foot Opening

Drill 1 Off the plate striding

In batting practice BP move off the plate and force yourself to stride towards either short stop or second base depending which side you hit from. As you do this the hitter is to feel his/her lead shoulder and hip staying closed because of the stride direction.

Drill 2 2x4 board

Put a 2x4 four (4) feet long behind the hitters back and lead foot heels. The board is to be pointing towards the pitcher. This makes it impossible for the hitter to stride anywhere but towards the pitcher.

Problem: Over striding

Drill 1

Cut down the effort or aggressiveness of the swing. This will slow up the pace of the hitter's strides. Start at the same effort as pepper, then go to fifty (50%) to seventy percent (70%) and so on until you can reach hundred percent (100%) while still striding short.

Drill 2 Lift up and set down

The front foot is lifted up and set down near the same place. The action of the lifting replaces the action of going out towards the pitcher. It is important when doing this drill to have your conscious mind concentrating on the lifting action.

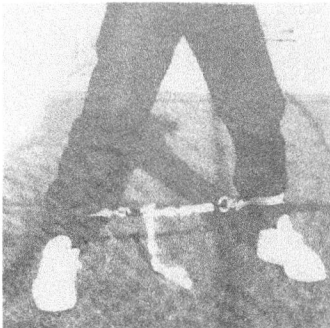

Drill 3 Stride Tudor or stride box

The stride Tudor is a device consisting of a plastic chain which attaches to each ankle with Velcro straps. Its purpose is to restrict the length of the stride by adjusting the length of the chain. The stride box is a box five feet by three feet (5'x3') that the hitter stands in while hitting. The length of the stride is restricted by an adjustable board which runs the width of the box.

Drill 4.

The hitter holds a ball between his/her legs just above the knees while taking flips.

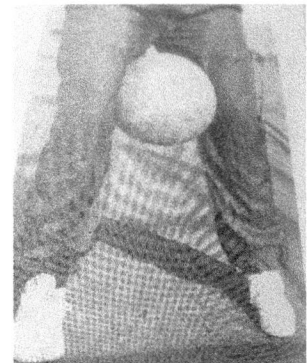

Drill 5 No stride hitting

The hitter takes flips and batting practice BP without striding.

Drill 6 Two concrete bloc The hitter's lead foot is blocked in with two concrete blocks. One behind the heel and one against the side of the foot. The hitter then hits without striding.

Problem Upper cutting

Drill 1 Over the ball swinging
  The hitter takes side or front flips while intentionally attempting to miss the ball by swinging over it. The hitter then progresses to hitting the top of the ball then to the middle of the ball.

Drill 2 Ground ball hitting The hitter attempts to hit the ball on the ground.

Drill 3 Target practice
  An object is set out in front of home plate fifteen (15) to twenty (20) feet. The hitter takes front flips with the mind set of hitting the object.

Drill 4 Chin to chin
  The hitter takes front flips starting with his/her chin on or near the front shoulder and finishing the swing with chin near the back shoulder.

Drill 5 Double tee
  Two tees are used. The first tee which holds the ball, is placed twelve (12) inches in front and slight lower than the back tee. The hitter then attempts to hit the ball without making contact with the back tee.

Drill 6 One knee drill
A. The hitter kneels on his/her front knee. Kneeling on the back knee causes the back shoulder to drop. The hitter holds the bat with his/her lead hand and chokes up about ten (10) inches. He/she then receives side flips concentrating on pulling the lead arm down and thru the swing. It is important to check to make sure the bat barrel is staying above the hands with the hands leading the barrel.

B. Put the top hand on the bat with an open hand. While pulling the bat with the lead arm use the top hand to push the bat.

C. Two handed swings concentrating on using the hands only. The hands should stay loose and quick. While doing this drill, feel how the back-shoulder stays when the bat is swung with the hands.

Drill 7 Back spin

The hitter takes side flips attempting to put back spin on the ball. His/her goal is to hit the ball to the back of the cage. If he/she is putting back spin on the ball he/she will feel that the proper way to start the swing is downward.

Drill 8 Hip popper

The hitter starts with the bat behind his/her back locked between his/her elbows. The bat barrel sticks out twelve (12) inches from his/her body. He/she then takes side flips while rotating the body and bat barrel down to the ball.

Drill 9 Mound flips

The hitter takes side flips while standing on downward angle of the mound. The hitter should get the feeling of working his/her swing down to the ball.

Problem: Long Swing and Casting

Drill 1 Fence swing (dry swings or front flips)

The hitter sets up in their stance standing twenty-four (24) inches to the left or right of fence or cage netting. When he/she sets up their hands they should be fifteen (15) inches from the fence or netting. The hitter then takes dry swings or front flips controlling his/her early movements. The feeling should be pulling both hands into the slot which is inside the ball. If the bat touches the fence or netting the batter is flopping the bat barrel.

Drill 2 In and out tees

The hitter hits off of two tees. One tee is set on the inside corner; the other is set on the outside corner. (Important: set on the inside tee up approximately twenty (24) inches in front of the front thigh and the outside tee at the front thigh.) A ball is set on both tees. A coach stands behind the hitter and after the hitter triggers his/her swing he/she tells the hitter in or out. The hitter then hits the appropriate ball.

Drill 3 Inside the ball tees

Two tees are used. Tee one is set up slightly back and outside of tee two. The ball is set on tee one. The hitter hits the ball while not hitting tee two. This helps to develop a downward swing.

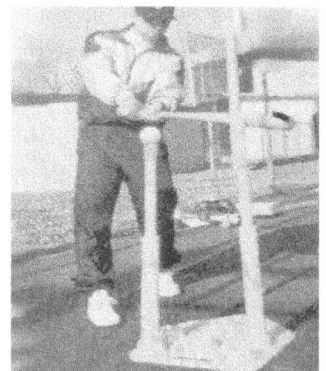

Drill 4 Other way flips

The hitter takes from flips with the mind set of hitting the ball the other way. The coach flips the ball on the inner half of the plate. Hitting the inside pitch, the other way forces the hitter to keep his/her hands inside the ball.

Drill 5 Angled flips

The hitter takes front flips from a thirty (30) degree angle. For a right-handed hitter the flipper will be thirty (30) degrees to the hitter's right. For the left-handed hitter he/she will be thirty (30) degrees to the hitter's left. Balls are flipped to the outside corner and the hitter goes with the ball the other way. This also develops a swing to hit the breaking ball.

Problem: Cutting off the Swing

Drill 1 Behind flips

A coach kneels ten (10) feet behind the hitter. The hitter turns his/her head and faces the coach. He/she tracks the ball and hits the ball out front with full arm extension. By hitting the ball before it gets out of reach force the hitter to extend his/her arms to the front position. After hitting the ball, it should continue on the same line

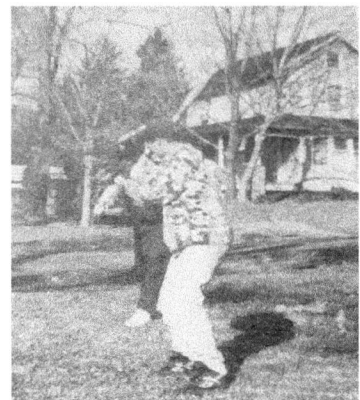

from which it was flipped. The coach can control the direction he/she wants the hitter to hit the ball. To do this change your angle of the pitch to the hitter.

Drill 2 Out front tee

The tee is set up slightly more than normal out in front of the plate. This forces the hitter to get his arms fully extended. To keep the hitter from getting out in front have him hit without a stride.

Drill 3 Double tee

Set up two balls on the tees directly behind each other. The hitter hits though the first ball and hits the second ball. His/her mind set is to hit past the first ball to the second. This helps him/her to feel the bat as well as to stay in the strike zone and on the ball longer.

Drill 4 Bat Throw

The hitter takes his/her normal stance and throws the bat up the middle. The release of the bat is made after the arms get fully extended. This will help him/her feel extension and what it feels like to hit the ball out front.

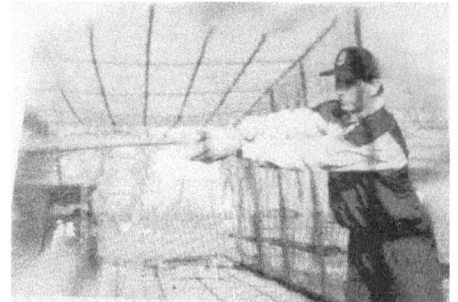

Problem: Head Pulling

Drill 1 Colored balls

The hitter takes side flips, front flips or batting practice using colored balls. The object is the hitter tracks the ball with his/her eyes and identifies the color of the ball.

Drill 2 Finger tees

The coach puts the ball on the tee. As the hitter swings, the coach puts down their finger from one to five. The hitter tells the coach how many fingers he/she puts down.

Drill 3 Knuckle ball flips

The hitter takes side flips with spin. The coach flips a knuckle ball and the object is to identify whether the hitter hit a seam or the white part of the ball.

Drill 4 Hat in front of plate

A hat is placed five (5) feet in front of home plate. Using a front flip <u>only</u>, the hitter tracks and hits the ball. Just after contact is made the hitter's eyes drop to the button on the cap. This also teaches the hitter that contact is always made from the front high forward.

Drill 5 Head still drill

The hitter gets into his/her stance and the coach puts his/her hand on top of the hitter's head. While the hitter strides he/she holds his/her head in place. This drill should be done both with the hitter striding long and short to show him/her the reaction of the head to each stride.

Problem: Loading or Trigger Swing

Drill 1 Golf Swing

The hitter takes dry swings using his/her golf swing. Starting from the address position in golf, swing the bat back to the baseball hitting launch position. This backward swinging action teaches the hitter to load his/her body weight to the rear leg.

Drill 2 Rhythm System

The purpose of this drill is to give the hitter the feeling that if he/she shifts their weight back slowly and relaxed, they will approach the ball in the same manner. This creates a rhythm or pace to the striding action. The drill starts with the weight on the front foot (picture 1 below) and the bat hanging forward near the front foot. As the ball is flipped the hitter drags the bat into the launch position. At the same time the body weight shifts to the rear leg (picture 2 below). As the bat and weight is shifted back the hitter immediately strides and swings the bat (picture 3 below). The drill is done slowly and relaxed giving the hitter the feeling he/she doesn't have to rush or jump at the ball.

1   2   3

Drill 3 Bat throw

The hitter takes his/her normal stance and throws the bat up the middle. The release of the bat is made after the arms get fully extended. This will help him/her feel extension and what it feels like to hit the ball out front. (Same as in cutting off the swing.)

Problem: Lunging

Drill 1 Stride separation flips

The hitter receives front flips while separating the swing and the stride. The hitter loads their body weight to his/her rear leg then strides while holding his/her weight back. The ball is not flipped until the stride is completed. Most of his/her body weight should be back when his/her front foot touches the ground. The hitter should be in control of their upper body and head. Watch for the head and body floating forward toward the pitcher. This floating action means the hitter is carrying the weight to the front foot too soon.

Drill 2

This drill is the same as the stride separation except the flipper fakes a flip to check the hitter's position after the striding action. The flipper can flip the ball out of the strike zone to work on his/her ball strike recognition. This teaches the hitter that it is easier to judge balls and strikes when he/she doesn't lunge.

Last message on drills

All of these drills can and will help learn and perfect the hitting mechanics but it takes dedication and practice. The desire to improve must be instilled in the youth as early as possible. Use these drills and words of encouragement to help the hitter build confidence and determination. They will also help you see the ball better to help with strike zone discipline. You will both come away feeling rewarded knowing that you're working to become better and appreciating the beauty of life.

Notes:

Baseball Statistics

Baseball statistics play an <u>important role</u> in evaluating the progress of a player and team.

They provide managers and players a record of how they are doing and improving over the course of the baseball season. Statistics are used to measure batting, baserunning, pitching, fielding, overall player value, and for general statistics. There are a ton of statistics that are available we'll just give the basic ones here.

Batting – The measurement to evaluate a hitter's success as a hitter.
There are a number of statistics to measure a hitter's success but the basic core is batting average, RBI, and homerun.
  a. **BA** Batting Average: Divide the number of hits by number of at bats. 5 for 10 = .500
  b. **RBI** is Run Batted In: Is the number of runners scored by hitter's by getting a base hit, sacrifice fly, walk, and any other way, except hitting into a double play or reach by an error.
  c. **HR** Home Run: Are the number of times a hitter touches all four bases with an at-bat without a fielding error.

Baserunning – The measurement of a runner's ability to steal a base.
  a. **SB** Stolen Base: The number of bases a runner steals when the defense has the ball.
  b. **CS** Caught Stealing: The number of times caught stealing when trying to steal a base.
  c. **SBA** or **ATT** – Stolen Base Attempts: Number of times a player attempted to steal a base.
  d. **SB%** Stolen Base Percentage: The percent of successfully steals. Stolen bases divided by attempts.

Pitching – The measurement of success a pitcher is pitching.
  a. **BB** Base on Balls (Walks): The four balls to hitter that put hitter on first base.
  b. **BF** Number of Batters Faced: Plate appearances of other team faced by pitcher in a game.
  c. **ERA** Earn Runs Average: The number of earned runs multiplied by 9, then divided by total innings pitched. Example: 5 earn runs, 20- innings pitched. 5x9=45/20=2.25 ERA

d. **L** Losses: The number of games while pitching the opposing team took the lead and went on to win the game.

e. **W** Wins: The number of games the team took a lead when pitching and team went on to win.

There are many more baseball statistics that are available to measure all parts of the game. If you are interested in finding more of the statistics you can find them in *"The Complete Encyclopedia of Baseball"* by Hy Turkin published in 1951, *"Baseball Encyclopedia"*, and *"Total Baseball"*

Notes:

_____
_____
_____
_____
_____
_____
_____
_____
_____
_____
_____
_____
_____
_____
_____
_____
_____
_____
_____
_____
_____
_____
_____
_____
_____
_____
_____
_____

Becoming a Pro
By Bob Braun

Steve Braun: Pinch-hitter deluxe, Doctor Stroke

These are some of the names Steve has earned because of his ability to deliver a key pinch hit when a game is on the line. Steve developed his skills as a pinch hitter early in his career when he played in the sand lots as a child.

Many of the other young ball players he played with would go to the ball field because there was nothing else to do or because their parents kicked them out of the house. Steve was different, he went to the ball field to play baseball. He loved the game, he loved the feeling he felt when the ball made contact with the bat, and he loved being a baseball player.

Steve has said many times, "I don't ever remember not wanting to be a professional baseball player". He was one of those lucky ones, who knew what he wanted to be at a very young age. He went to the sand lot not to waste time, but to practice and develop his skills in fielding, hitting, and running. He went to the ball field because he loved the game of baseball.

Steve played Little League, Babe Ruth, and American Legion. He also played baseball in grammar school and high school. In every stage of his development Steve played with a great deal of intensity and worked to improve in the game he loved. He listened to his coaches and watched his fellow players. Always willing to learn something. Always willing to improve his skills.

In 1966, after graduating from high school Steve was drafted in the eleventh round by the Minnesota Twins. Steve was sent to the Sarasota Twins in Florida, the Twins Gulf Coast rookie affiliate. In his first year at Sarasota Steve was anything but successful. He hit only 230 with no homeruns.

Steve did not get discouraged but continued to work hard in the off-season. He signed another contract with the Twins and started the 1967 season with the Sarasota Twins. He was assigned to the Twins affiliate that played at Wisconsin Rapids after the Gulf Coast League season was completed.

After Steve's second year in professional baseball, he was drafted into the Army. Getting drafted into the Army may have been the most influential event to affect his baseball career. The army matured Steve, changing him from a boy to a

man, more determined to achieve his goal of becoming a professional baseball player. He was lucky enough to be stationed in Germany where he was able to play baseball. In his second year in the Army, he was named all-star shortstop for the All-Europe Championship baseball team.

Steve was discharged from the Army on September 23, 1969. He played semi-pro before he went to play winter ball in Florida. This is when Steve began to show his potential.

Due to his maturity and his increase in self-confidence, Steve used his skills developed during his youth to hit 304. This impressed many because Steve not only hit 304 against the most promising young prospects in baseball, but he achieved it after being out of the Army for only two months.

The following summer Steve was sent to Lynchburg Virginia, where Steve had an excellent year. He ended up hitting 279 with 43 RBIs and 4 homeruns after a slow start. He was also voted to the Carolina League all-stars team. Steve was finally showing the baseball world that he had the tools to be a winner. He never forgot the importance of working hard and learning by watching and listening to others.

He would always be one of the first on the ball field and last to leave. Steve learned in the Army that there are people of authority that make decisions and they must be impressed. So, he worked hard to impress these people of authority, but, more importantly, he was sharpening and developing his skills. He wanted to be a professional baseball player.

During the winter of 1970 Steve was again asked to play winter ball in Florida. He had another impressive season. Steve showed the baseball people that as the competition improved so did his average.

His performance was so impressive that he was invited to Minnesota's 1971 Spring Training Camp. This was an unusual achievement, because only the top 40 ball players in the entire Minnesota organization are invited to the Spring Training Camp, and Steve had only played for Minnesota's, single A, minor league team.

In the spring of 1971 Steve had his biggest break in baseball. Ron Carew the regular second baseman for Minnesota had dental problems. This provided Steve an opportunity to have more playing time than he or anyone expected.

Pencil drawing by brother Rich.

Steve responded like the pro he is, exceeding all expectations by hitting 334 in Spring Training and playing a superb second base. He made the Minnesota's Twins 25-man roster that Spring to begin his long and successful 15-year major league career.

During Steve's fifteen years career Steve played with the Minnesota Twins, Seattle Mariners, Toronto Blue Jays, Kansas City Royals, and with the St. Louis Cardinals the final five years. He played in one American League play-offs with the Kansas City Royals. He also played in the 1982 and 1985 World Series as a member of the St. Louis Cardinals.

Steve walked in the game's winning run in the second game of the 1982 World Series that pitted the Cardinals against the Milwaukee Brewers. He finished this series with a 500-batting average. He drove in two runs in helping St. Louis beat the Milwaukee Brewers in seven games in what was called the series between the beer capitals of the world.

Steve earned the nickname Pinch-Hitter Deluxe, because of his uncanny ability to come into the late inning game, and deliver a key pitch hit or earn a base on balls.

During the pennant drive in the 1985 season Steve hit a pinch-hit two run homer in the tenth inning to win the ball game against the Dodgers. This key pinch-hit homerun kept the Cardinals a half game up on the New York Mets. The very next day Steve singled in another game winning run to extend the Cardinals lead over the Mets by a game and a half. These two key pinch-hits helped the Cardinals win their division in 1985 by only a two-game margin.

Throughout Steve's successful career he has always been known as a great natural hitter. But it was in the last six or seven years that Steve was able to learn and develop his philosophy of hitting. During this time Steve began to be known as a player who had the skills and mental ability to come off the bench to deliver a key pinch-hit.

Coming cold off the bench to pinch hit is one of the hardest things to do in baseball. Just imagine being asked to come off the bench, go to the batter's box, and hit against a pitcher that may be throwing at a speed of up to or over a hundred miles per hour. Not only are you going up to the plate cold but may not have hit or played in a game for a week or two.

It takes a special disciplined player that has control of their mind and knows and understands the philosophy of hitting. He must spend extra time in the batting cage to simulate the game, and use the time he is waiting to prepare himself mentally and physically. He must realize that the team is the most important thing and to win as a team. He must study and analyze other hitters and know the opposition pitchers. All of this to kill time and be ready to come off the bench to pinch-hit, usually with the game in a win or lose situation. All of these qualities can be summed up in two words, *Steve Braun*.

Steve was only the tenth player in the history of baseball to have had a hundred pinch-hits or more, finishing with113 pinch-hits. He retired from baseball in sixth place on the all-time pinch-hit list, only three pinch-hits behind Jerry Lynch who is in 4th place. It is quite an accomplishment considering how many ballplayers that had played professional baseball.

Steve always was and still is a student of hitting. He watched and played with some of the best hitters that ever played the game of baseball. Some of these players include Harmon Killebrew, Tony Oliva, Ron Carew, George Brett, Keith Hernandez, Jack Clark and so many more.

He always tried to learn from the great hitters he played with. He tried to break down the swing of these great hitters to determine why they were so good. What he saw and learned he applied to his swing and his philosophy of hitting.

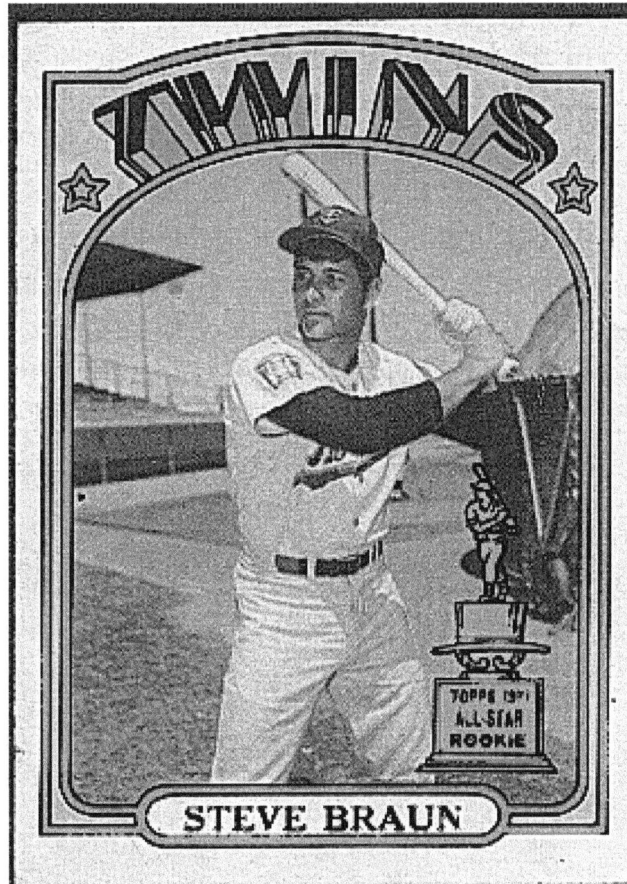

Steve's major league career began in 1971 as the third baseman for the Minnesota Twins. In his first year Steve's batting average was 254 and he was voted to the Baseball Digest Rookie All-Star Teams, as the best rookie third baseman.

In his second year Steve hit 289 with 50 RBIs. He also played four positions in the field and had his first of seven consecutive 100 or more hit seasons.

He continued to excel as a player. In 1974 he hit 302 for the season, tenth in the American League, and had a career high of 11 homeruns. The following year Steve had a career high of 61 RBIs while batting 289 for the season.

At the end of the 1976 season Steve was selected by Seattle Mariners in the American League Expansion Draft. He played two years with Seattle and was traded to Kansas City Royals for pitcher Jim Colborn on June 1, 1979.

While playing with Kansas City he set a club record for being on base eleven times in a row. Steve still holds the record for the most pinch-hits as a Cardinal.

Steve ended his professional career with a 271-batting average and ended having 989 hits during his stay in the big leagues. He retired in 1986 a victim of the reduction of the team's roster from 25 men to 24.

After his retirement Steve was the hitting instructor for the Cardinals before moving on to the Boston Red Sox's and Yankees minor league. The job of hitting instructor is a position that Steve was comfortable in. He has the ability to communicate with younger ball players and his knowledge helps them relax. By being relaxed they can apply many of his instructions while hitting in a game.

Steve's success in baseball is contributed to his natural ability and his dedication to making himself better. To never be satisfied, but to reach out to make himself a better hitter as well as a better person. With this self-drive Steve is insured success in anything he does because he applies many of his basic hitting philosophy, to his basic philosophy of life.

STEVE BRAUN
Seattle MARINERS
OUTFIELD

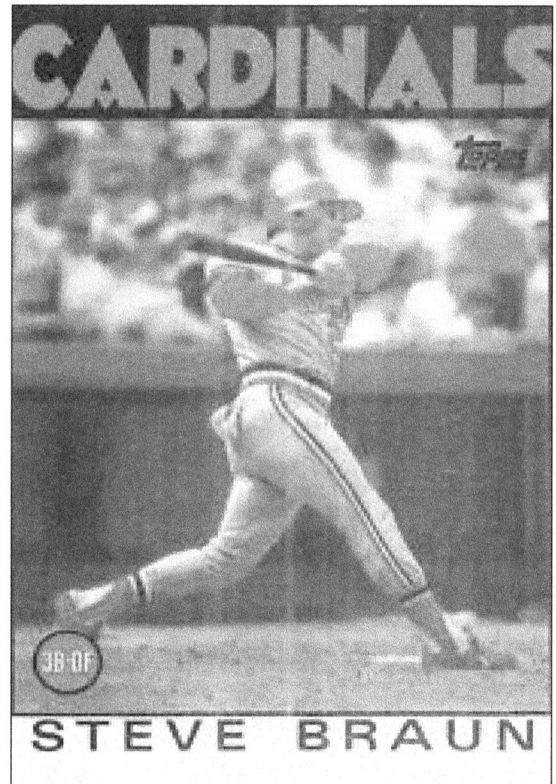

CARDINALS
3B-OF
STEVE BRAUN

+

| **Rich** | **Bob** | **Steve** |

The Brothers

This is a picture of Steve, Rich, and Bob before a game at Old Yankee Stadium. Rich and Bob were able to take turns using one of Steve's uniforms to shag fly balls during warm ups and visit the plaques and monuments in center field. All three were successful: Steve with his baseball. Richard with his Art. and Bob with his writing.

The Brothers' Story

The three brothers Steve, Rich, and Bob grew up in the small town of Titusville and lived in a place called Washington Crossing. They are the oldest of nine children four boys and five girls. Steve is the oldest born nine months one day before identical twins Rich and Bob. Rich was born ten minutes before Bob and was the heaviest weighing three pounds fifteen ounces and Bob three pounds thirteen ounces.

They spent many hours growing up playing basketball and baseball in their back yard and neighborhood. All three played Little League, Babe Ruth baseball and varsity basketball for their high school. Steve went on to play high school varsity baseball and was drafted after high school. He went on to play fifteen years in the major league then coach in the minor league for a number of years as indicated in the story about him, "**Becoming a Pro**". Rich and Bob went on to play years of slow pitch softball. All three were successful because they wanted to be good by practicing the game they loved to play. Always first to practice and last to leave and playing the game as if they had a one run lead no matter the score, helped all three have successful sports careers.

Rich was also a great artist that was featured on covers of national magazines, see the following part about Rich. Rich was a pitcher that at one time was one of the best around. If you place the box the softball came in on the plate Rich could throw a high ark pitch right into the box.

Their practice field, when growing up, was/is an old school yard at the old Titusville grammar school overlooking the Delaware River. Here is a story by Bob that are in a number of his books about the old practice field where they practiced with their dad. Bob also used the field to practice with his daughters Kim, Emily, and son Rob.

The Old School Yard

by Bob Braun

Take me out to the old ball field, echoes on the red bricks of the old school. Hopefully another pro will outgrow the fences that were out of reach not long ago.

Many feet have run across the aged green grass that still makes a good field. There goes another pitch of many buckets of balls that have seen the face of the bat, too many to count.

Years ago, working with my brothers, waiting for my turn to hit, I can still remember enjoying them having fun. How I've enjoyed watching us all grow living different lives but remaining the same. How proud I am to have them play with my kids.

The field would be proud of the success lived by many laughing children that fell, cried and loved being free to run on it; still here to help me develop the next pro that may come out of the old ball field.

One of the things that helped the three become the athletes they became was, their work ethics and the competition between them. To help build strength their father bought a five-spring exercise apparatus that they used every night to build muscle, starting with one spring and moved on to using all five springs.

They also did jumps every night to increase their jumping ability. First the door way then eventually the ceiling. Their mother always complained about hand prints on the ceiling.

Carl, the brothers' younger brother known as the "Shark", won the NJ baseball state championship beating Lenape Valley High School 3 to 1. His team had a record of 20 wins and 6 losses in his senior year in high school as the shortstop and leadoff hitter. Competition and playing with his older brothers helped him develop his skills. He was called the Shark because of the way he gobbled up ground balls at short stop.

Bob's son Rob, was also a great ball player. He won the batting title his senior year with an average of four fifty-five (.455) and made all area. This was impressive since his league ended up winning two state championships in baseball that year.

Baseball has been a big part of the Braun family and continues to be.

Bob used the information in "Hitting Drills and Much More" to help him manage his son's Rob's Babe Ruth 12-year all-stars to a district championship.

The hitting drills and all the information in "Hitting Drills and Much More" helped Bob's son Rob achieve success by winning the batting title with a batting average of 455 and making the All-area Baseball First Team for the year 2000.

BATTING
(MINIMUM OF 50 AT-BATS)

Player	School	G	AB	H	AVG.
Rob Braun	Hopewell Valley	21	66	30	.455
			71	32	.451

FINAL COLONIAL VALLEY CONFERENCE STATISTIC

BATTING
(MINIMUM OF 50 AT-BATS)

Player	School	G	AB	H	AVG.
Rob Braun	Hopewell Valley	21	66	30	.455
Brian Hollows	West Windsor	23	71	32	.451
Matt Giannacio	Hamilton	31	107	47	.439
Rich Canuso	Steinert	27	71	30	.423
Mike Costello	McConislh	21	59	24	.407
Tom Sweeney	McConislh	20	59	24	.407
Tom Lee	Trenton	21	50	20	.400
Juan Gomez	Hopewell Valley	18	63	25	.397
Ian McGee	Steinert	27	54	21	.389
Paul Bendiverga	Hamilton	30	90	35	.389
Paz Zegarski	Lawrence	22	57	26	.368
Eric Weiner	Steinert	30	104	40	.385
Joe Hernandez	Notre Dame	21	55	21	.382
Paul Ryan	West Windsor	23	53	20	.377
Josh High	Steinert	32	96	36	.375
Chris Talar	Hopewell Valley	23	59	22	.373
Jim Massaro	Steinert	31	94	35	.372
Sean Whalen	Nottingham	25	73	27	.370
Eric Bruhn	Notre Dame	23	73	27	.370
Adam Priest	Hightstown	16	54	20	.370
Dave Schierholz	Steinert	30	61	30	.370
Steve Fischer	Steinert	27	76	28	.368
Scott Rich	Hamilton	31	93	34	.360
Nick Massari	Lawrence	22	73	26	.361
Kyle Anderson	Princeton	22	64	23	.359
Matt Ross	Steinert	27	54	19	.352
Joe Wynoski	Princeton	20	54	19	.352
Kevin Graydon					

Bob Blondage	Lawrence	22	84	26	.310
Adam Allen	Nottingham	23	71	22	.310
Kyle Hutchinson	West Windsor	23	55	17	.309
Erwin Barrientos	Nottingham	27	59	18	.305
Bill Seiler	Steinert	30	66	20	.303
Chris Freihaut	Notre Dame	23	86	26	.303
James Hoey	Hamilton	31	83	25	.301

HITS
Matt Giannacio, Hamilton	47	
Joe Hernandez, Steinert	40	
Chris Talar, Steinert	36	
Paul Ryan, Notre Dame	5	
Bob Ziegler, Steinert	5	

RUNS BATTED IN
Matt Giannacio, Hamilton	47
Pat Zegarski, Hamilton	35
Bob Ziegler, Steinert	34
Sean Whalen, Steinert	35
Scott Rich, Steinert	31
Nick Massari, Hamilton	34
Scott Senese, Hamilton	33
Brian Hollows, West Windsor	32
Pat Zegarski, Hamilton	28
Rob Braun, Hopewell Valley	30
Rob Braun, Hopewell Valley	28

RUNS SCORED
Mike Costello, Steinert	30
Chris Talar, Steinert	49
Steve Fischer, Steinert	30
Nick Massari, Hamilton	38

DOUBLES
Joe Hernandez, Steinert	37
Pat Zegarski, Hamilton	11
Scott Rich, Steinert	33
Matt Giannacio, Hamilton	11
Scott Senese, Hamilton	33
Scott Senese, Hamilton	9
Nick Massari, Hamilton	8
Bob Ziegler, Steinert	31
Adam Allen, Nottingham	8

STOLEN BASES
Chris Talar, Steinert	18
Pat Shipe, Hamilton	14

TRIPLES
Joe Hernandez, Steinert	3
Tom Hopkins, Hightstown	11
Brian Hollows, West Windsor	11
Earl Bradford, Ewing	5
Matt Barrett, Hopewell Valley	11
Scott Senese, Hamilton	4
Jon Meszaros, Hopewell Valley	11
Eric Weiner, Lawrence	4
William Johnson, Trenton	10

ALL-AREA BASEBALL
FOR YEAR 2000
FIRST TEAM

Position	Player	School	Class
Infield	Matt Giannacio	Hamilton	Senior
Infield	Nick Massari	Hamilton	Soph.
Infield	Joe Hernandez	Steinert	Senior
Infield	Rich Canuso	Notre Dame	Senior
Outfield	Chris Talar	Steinert	Senior
Outfield	Mark Reiter	Hunterdon Central	Senior
Outfield	Jake Serfass	Pennsbury	Senior
Catcher	Mike Zambriczki	Council Rock	Senior
Catcher	Sean Whalen	Steinert	Senior
Pitcher	Jim Hoey	Hamilton	Senior
Pitcher	Mike Rogers	Steinert	Junior
Pitcher	Dan Farino	Rancocas Valley	Senior
Pitcher	Adam Hanson	Lawrenceville	Senior
DH	Rob Braun	Hopewell Valley	Senior
Utility	L. B. Mentz	Lawrenceville	Senior

Baseball continues to be a big part of the Brauns' family now Steve's and Bob's grandsons are playing and loving the game of baseball.

Andrew Bob's grandson first game.

Andrew Bob's grandson at age of eleven.

Ryder Steve's youngest grandson.

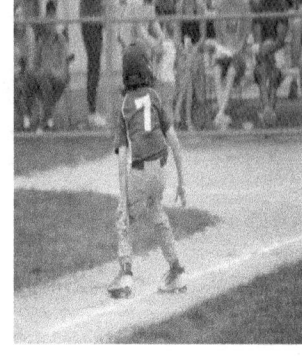

Dylan Steve's oldest grandson.

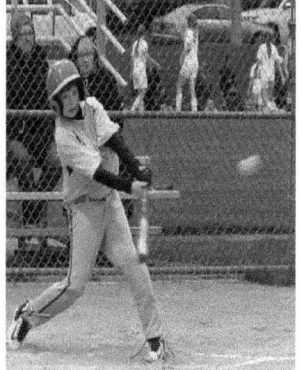

Steve Russell Braun

Much about Steve can be learned by reading the story "**Becoming a Pro**" if you have not already read his story. The story tells what helped make Steve a professional baseball player and could help another ball player become a pro.

Steve is presently retired from baseball. He has spent enjoying his retirement years traveling around the country visiting his son, Steven, his daughter Erin, and his grandchildren.

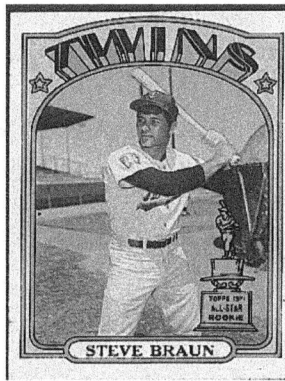

Steve as the hitting instructor for the Boston Red Sox's

Richard Joseph Braun

This is a portion of the book dedicated to Rich.
Many of the pictures included in this book are done by Rich.

The following are some art pieces by Richard
that shows the beauty of life.

Steve's younger brother and Bob's (my) twin
Brother.

**To honor him best is to let you see his love of life
though the beauty of his art.**

Rich "Dickaloo"

Rich passed away on November 26, 2013 after a long battle with what was thought to be, Alzheimer/ Frontotemporal Dementia. His passing has left an empty spot in both Steve's and Bob's heart.

This is what was written in a local paper.
"Richard J. Braun of Ewing, has been accepted into God's loving embrace on Tuesday, November 26, 2013, at Royal Health Gate of Lawrenceville with his loving wife by his side" Dickaloo," as he was affectionately referred to by his family and friends, was born in Trenton on February 9, 1949 and was a lifelong area resident, Dickaloo was a self-taught artist who enjoyed the outdoors, fishing, and playing softball with his brothers. He was an avid Yankees fan and sports enthusiast who cheered on Notre Dame football and Duke basketball. Dickaloo loved the beauty of life which inspired him to create art."

Color pencil drawing Rich did of his
oldest daughter Liz.

Rich also has another daughter Alex,
who played on a travel softball team
in her area growing up.

Both of these oils are of the Delaware River at Washington Crossing, NJ where in 1776 George Washington and his loyal men crossed the Delaware on a cold Christmas night on their way to independence. The fisherman in **"A *Good Day"*** is just south of the bridge shown below. From the story **"*Pass the Worms*"** in the book **"*Moral Duty"*.**

All three of these drawings are pencil that tells a story in themselves. Togetherness and love will eventually win but it is always easier with good memories. The above drawings are in the story *"Look Who Is Wearing the Apron"* and the drawing below is called *"Friendship"*. It is brother Steve with his manager Whity Herzog as they were on their way to winning the 1982 World Series. It is in the story *"Becoming A Pro."*

This is a pastel on velvet above showing a young girl with her best friend at Christmas. It is in the story **"Christmas Morning"** in the book **"Moral Duty"**.

These are color pencil drawings by Rich. Above is Steve and Derek Jeter at third base at a Trenton Thunder game when Derek was rehabbing after an injury and below fans enjoying a game.

This is a color pencil drawing of a young ball player getting ready to step to the plate. This moment a hitter must have confidence in themself. Confidence comes from working hard and smart.

The cover of this book.

These are oil Paintings

**Taken September 11, 2002 at the Newark, NJ
YMCA when it was unveiled.
It is a large oil painting that has the word LOVE
hidden throughout the painting.**

Robert Mark Braun, Sr.

A year after high school Bob was drafted into the Army Infantry, and was sent to Vietnam where he was severely wounded in ground action. He is a disabled Vietnam Veteran who received two Purple Hearts, a Bronze Medal for Bravery, and was awarded the New Jersey Distinguished Service Medal in 2000.

After he was released from the Army on September 1, 1970, he graduated from Rider College with a Bachelor of Science in Commerce and a minor in accounting degree in February 1977. He then worked for thirty-four-years as an auditor for the NJ State Treasury Department specializing in Inheritance and Estate tax, and has been retired since May 1, 2010.

During this time, he self-published the first addition of this book in 1996 and the book titled, "A Story of Life" in 2000. He had to give up marketing the books because he had to raise his children as a single parent. Bob had to make a choice between his books or children. It wasn't a hard choice; he chose his kids.

Bob coached and managed his son Rob's and his daughters Kim's and Emily's basketball and baseball/softball teams, and studied major league coaches Steve played under, all helped him develop his philosophies for his writings on the **"Art of Coaching"**. After retirement he worked on and completed the second edition, now the third edition of this book, along with the book "Two Times Dead in Vietnam", and "Moral Duty". He has also published four children's books, they are "What is Cool Puppy Doing?", "The Bug Book", "Billy Likes the River", and "What is Georgie Doing?".

The best way for you to know Bob is to read some of the stories from his books. Hopefully, you have already read the story about Steve in **"Becoming a Pro"** and **"The Old School Yard"**, and read about Rich and reviewed his art that showed his love of life. The following are samples of his books. The next story by Bob is about his first year of being Mr. Mom.

LOOK WHO'S WEARING THE APRON
by Bob Braun

I am a middle-aged jock who is in my second year of being Mr. Mom, changing positions with my ex-wife by taking over primary physical custody of two minor children. No big deal, it's happening more and more often in today's world of the 90's where men are accepting the responsibility of caring for their children.

My story starts on December 15, 1993 by moving back into the marital home, after over two and half years of living in a one-bedroom apartment and being an-every other weekend Mr. Mom. I had high expectations of molding my kids into highly efficient on time machines. I was so sure of my persuasive skills that I totally over looked that I was dealing with a twelve-year-old boy, and a nine-year-old girl who lived with me, while my older daughter stayed with my ex-sister-in-law. I entered a new life with confidence believing the household, would be running smoothly in a very short time, and was determined to change things by making my home a perfect environment.

Pencil drawing of Bob's three children by Rich.

Being a morning person, who normally got five or six hours of sleep and in great shape, I saw the everyday responsibilities of washing clothes, doing dishes, and preparing meals as only a slight inconvenience of my everyday routine as a non-mother. I couldn't imagine myself becoming discouraged or sorry about becoming a full-time single parent. There was no way I was going to allow two little kids to stop me from reaching my goals.

While growing up in a large family, I watched my mother labor over scrub board or old wringer washing machine, washing diaper after diaper for nine children. I was confident that I could manage only two kids in a home with all the modern conveniences of the nineties. I've survived the Army and jungles of Viet Nam so I believed there would be no problem training two out of control kids.

It was unbelievable, that after only three months I knew what it meant by the saying, being a mother is a thankless job. I abandoned my belief that the kids would be easily molded into self-efficient responsible kids. Instead, I was rudely awakened to the fact that any change would take time and a lot more patience than I knew was possible.

I found out what dishpan hands were all about. I also came to understand that for some reason there are always dishes in the sink and that the dryer eats socks, not both socks, but only one of a matching pair. I continued to try, after folding the clothes, to match the single socks with the ever-growing bag of matchless socks and have experienced the joy of finding a match. It easily over shadows the joy of catching a winning touchdown or hitting a game winning grand slam, things I used to think were so important.

Quickly giving up my ideology of using my concept of allowance as a manipulating tool to get my two kids to do their chores, make their lunches and beds, and be nice to each other. Instead, I found myself doing exactly what I used to criticize my ex-wife and mother for doing, just doing things myself instead of battling the kids. It was just easier doing things myself than trying to make them and damn it; I knew it was wrong.

I don't know why but I kept hearing myself say things I never accepted before like: "I'm tired of doing everything." "You kids better start appreciating what I'm doing for you" or, "You guys better start helping because I can't do it all myself." I think what was happening was the fumes from the dish and laundry detergent was affecting my brain cells, causing me to lose my power. Maybe it was the sudden change in temperature between sticking my head in the refrigerator and standing over the hot oven. Possibly it was the dust of the vacuum cleaner and the lint from folding the clothes. Whatever it was, it was hard to distinguish the difference of being a Mr. Mom, from being a Mom. Sometimes, I would go to the bathroom and stand up, just to remember that I'm not a member of the so called, "weaker sex."

I've became aware of how little I appreciated a mother's job. The never-ending number of responsibilities, chores that must be done every day, and making sure everyone else's needs are taken care of before tending to your own. The stress of planning and then cooking meals that will be eaten, making sure everyone has clothes to wear, cleaning, and all the other jobs around the house. It's a job that's, never done!

I did have a few things going for me, like a great drive to succeed and an appreciation of life. Something learned while fighting in the jungles of Vietnam, where I had to fight for my life, plus the loss of my closest Vietnam friend, Jack Rae Smith while serving there. Every day I think about my experience in Vietnam and what my mother went through and use them to inspire me to continue to better myself, work hard, and, treasure what I have.

There was no way I was going to abandon my goals of teaching my kids the need to learn and take care of themselves. There was no way I was going to admit failure and give up. Lucky for me, I was already doing some things right.

Each weekend a dish or two was prepared for a quick meal during the week and there was always homemade spaghetti sauce for a pasta dish. Meals the kids liked were made so they would become confident with my cooking. Fatty foods or sweets were not found in the house and ready to cook hamburger patties that were mixed from ground turkey and lean hamburger meat were in the freezer.

At least one load of laundry was done almost every night, so it wouldn't be a major job. Most of my social life was doing things with the kids and free weekends were spent cleaning the house, working in the yard and gardens, and remodeling the home. Probably the smartest thing I did was start talking to women, asking them how they managed their home and then brought up my problems. Gradually, I began to pick up little bits of information to help me run my household.

Every night I began to pick up to make sure the house was in order before going to bed. I made sure the two kids did the few chores I assigned, was persistent in making sure they maintained proper sleeping habits, and seldom wavered in making sure we all stayed on schedule. Slowly routines were set, habits formed, and both kids started losing weight. My son started to swim without a tee shirt because he was no longer embarrassed about extra weight. I started receiving compliments on how much better the kids looked and behaved.

What helped most was enjoying the little victories, like being able to express my love, tucking them in each night, telling them I loved them, and hearing them respond that they loved me too. I told my kids that I was only human and make mistakes just like they do. We started to work as a team and I learned what motivated them. There were big enjoyments too, like my son excelling in baseball and learning to work hard to improve, my youngest daughter's self-improvements, and developing a closer relationship with my older daughter.

My youngest daughter had a learning disability so she was struggling in school. She was very cold towards me. I spent time with her and made sure she got into a habit of doing her homework as soon as she got home from school. Every night I would check her homework and if it wasn't correct, I would insist that it was done correctly.

Now she does her homework without me telling her, leaves it out for me to check, and doesn't complain when she has to correct a mistake.

Her confidence grew and she began feeling proud of herself. She has done so well she has been on the honor roll the first and second marking periods and got straight A's the third. **I couldn't have been prouder**. My patience and persistence of showing her love has melted the ice between us. She is involved in sports and is a happy lovable young lady, always ready for a hug and kiss.

My son had already been a good baseball player, and we spent many hours working on it, setting up a weight lifting program for him and he hit off the tee almost every night. By the time the season opened we were both aware of how much he had improved.

The baseball team he played on, and I coached, had come in last place the previous two years. The league was the strongest it had been in a long time with no dominating team.

What a year our team had. We went from last to first, winning the playoffs with a record of 17-1. My son hit close to 800 and had a pitching record of 12-1.

I went on to manage the 12-year-old All-stars. The team won the district championship and came in second and third in two other tournaments. My son was

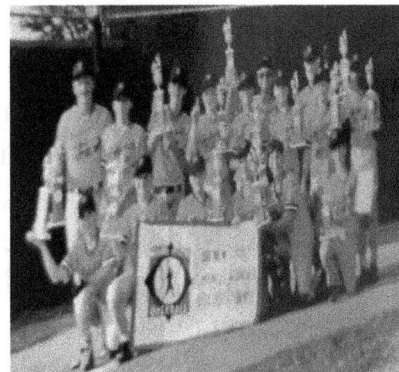

one of the top players, batting third and catching when he wasn't pitching.

Making it through the first year was a major accomplishment. I am now confident in my ability, as a Mr. Mom, that I'll be able to succeed in caring for my children. I am making sure the house is clean while still maintaining a full and part time job, coaching both baseball and basketball, writing, helping the kids in school, and all the many other jobs around the house. Many nights I go to bed tired but, there is always a smile on my face knowing I've created a stable, happy, and loving environment for my children. I now know that a mother's job is never done, and appreciate what it takes to be a single parent in the nineties.

Four Children's Books

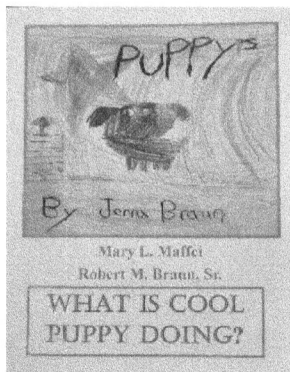

Retail book Price $13.99
Book is 8.5 x 11 inches.
ISBN: 978-1-890007-08-9

What is Cool Puppy Doing? is co-authored by my seven-year-old granddaughter, Jenna M. Braun and Mary L. Maffei. Picture on the cover by Jenna M. Braun.

What is Cool Puppy Doing? is designed for children: to help them learn to read, know shapes, numbers, colors, important signs, and their favorite vegetables and fruits, as well as giving the child a place to color and name the picture they color. This book is appropriate for the child in pre-school through fourth grade.

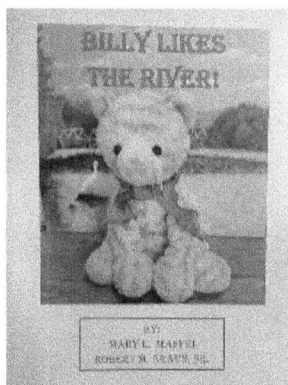

Retail book Price $13.99
Book is 8.5 x 11 inches.
ISBN: 978-1-890007-13-3

Billy Likes the River is co-authored by Mary L Maffei.

Billy Likes the River is an interactive book that is designed to advance and create the foundation for healthy learning and the development of the child. It helps the child learn the skills they need for life, like: communicating, thinking, problem-solving, and being with others.

The book starts with different activities by the river, moves to the names and pictured of birds, and much more. It helps the child to read aloud and sound out words, which are both educational social tools and skills needed by the young reader. The book introduces them to simple addition and encourages the young reader to use their fingers, if necessary, to help solve addition problems, all while being coached by their friend, Billy. The book *Billy Likes the River* provides encouragement to young readers to use their creativity skills to name the pictures they color. This book is appropriate for the child in pre-school through fourth grade.

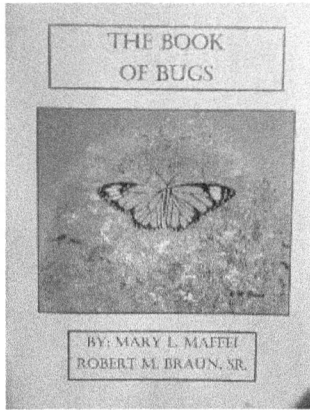

Retail book Price $13.99
Book is 8.5 x 11 inches.
ISBN: 978-1-890007-12-6

The Book of Bugs is co-authored by Mary L. Maffei.

The Book of Bugs is an educational tool to help the young reader, learn to read, the alphabet, count to fifty, sound out words, recognize street signs, name the planets, and build word vocabulary. The book is a delightful, beautifully illustrated interactive book that builds children's confidence in basic literacy and decision-making skills. It generates creative thinking while strengthening bonds with the parent, teacher, grandparent, and anyone reading with the child. It is an excellent book that would be welcome in any child's library. This book is appropriate for the child in pre-school through fourth grade.

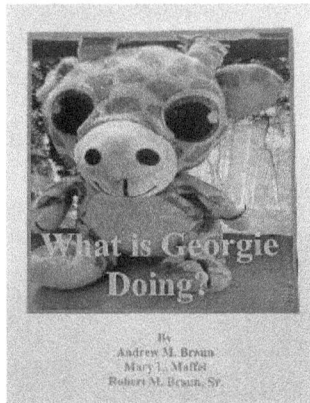

Retail book Price $13.99
Book is 8.5 x 11 inches.
ISBN: 978-1-890007-11-9

What is Georgie Doing? is co-authored by my nine-year-old grandson Andrew M. Braun and Mary L. Maffei.

What is Georgie Doing? is an interactive book that is designed to advance and create the foundation for healthy learning and the development of the child. It helps the more advanced child learn the skills they need for life, like communicating, thinking, problem-solving, and being with others. The book provides encouragement to young readers to use their creativity skills to name the pictures they color. This book is appropriate for the child in pre-school through fourth grade.

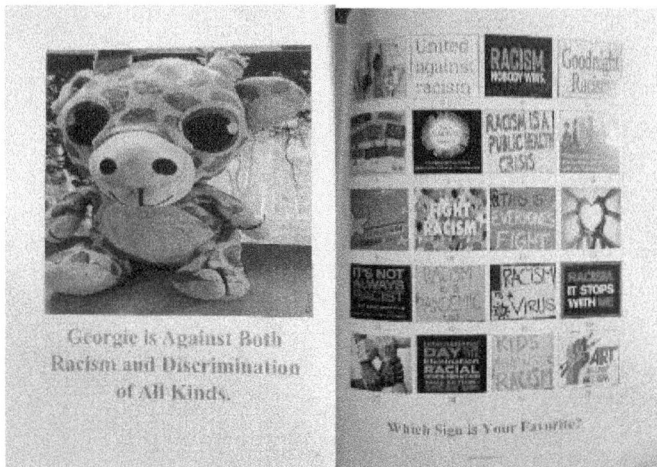

Georgie is Against
Both Racism and
Decimation of
All Kinds

"TWO TIMES DEAD IN VIETNAM"

by Robert M. Braun, Sr.

ISBN: 978-1-890007-06-5 (sc)
Retail price: $19.99
ISBN: 978-1-890007-25-6 (hc)
Retail price: $29.99

This is a story fifty years in the making. It is about some of my missions during the four months and eleven days I spent in Vietnam, how I was injured, and how my friend Jack Rae Smith lost his life. The book is organized into seven parts.

Some of the chapters included are: "Welcome to Vietnam", "Christmas New Years Eve", "The Bob Hope Christmas Show", "The Sun at Last", "Swimming in the Saigon River", "With Me Still," "First Last Rites", "Second Last Rites", "Going Home." There are also six newspaper articles, including "Robert Braun Proves You Can Fight City Hall."

Soldier Boy

Waste, waste, young soldier boy never return the same,
nightmares of human carrion like maggots eating flesh of
Boys ripped from wombs of home.
Heroes lined in black plastic bags, numbers for each night.
Protest at Kent State, Washington D C
Advance the cause of truth.
Let the souls beyond the graves protect
our future youth.

This poem is dedicated to **Jack Rae Smith** and all those that made the ultimate sacrifice for our country and democracy.

Moral Duty

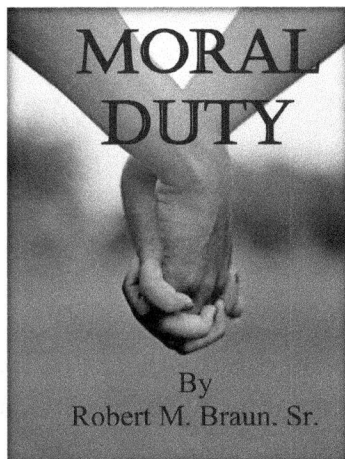

ISBN: 978-1-890007-16-4 (e)
eBook: $9.00
ISCN 987-1-89000-19-5 (sc)
Softcover: $19.00
ISBN: 978-1-890007-27-0 (hcbw)
Hardcover: $39.99

The book is a collection of writings over the years of performing my moral duty, to fight for truths and against injustice to help advance our world to a better future, while providing a wealth of information in captivating stories: topics range from raising three children as a single parent, to losing my identical twin brother to dementia. The book includes stories entitled "Equal Employment for the Disabled", "Look Who's Wearing the Apron", "The Importance of Amino Acids", "Dementia/Alzheimer", "Flat Tax Not Fair", "King's Puppets", "The Nurse the Giver", stories about cancer, autism, givers, greed, Machiavellianism, and has thirty-seven letters that were published in local newspapers. All of these writings are in chapters titled **"Moral Duty/Moral Responsibility"**, **"Power of the Pen"**, **"Diet and Health"**, and **"The Love of Life"**. These are samples from the book *"Moral Duty"*.

Freedom

Printed in Trenton Times, October 2002

I am writing in regards to the article, "Protesters Register Their Point of View From Afar", in the September 24, 2002 Trenton Times. What struck me the most about the article is not the protesters but what was said about them by the Bush supporters. In particular what was said by Art Ward of Bensalem, PA, when he said, "They should shoot them." Where is the freedom guaranteed in our Constitution when one cannot have conflicting beliefs? Mr. Ward should be arrested and put on trial for terroristic and threatening remarks.

There is no place in a free democracy for one side of an issue to resort to violence if another disagrees with them. All violence must stop because violence only leads to more violence. This will happen more and more as one party continues to increase its power and resort to arrogance by refusing to respect other opinions.

(One example of the thirty-seven-letters published in Trenton Times included in "Moral Duty".)

More In Life

I saw and came close to death;
it is why I do more in life.

Say:

A picture is worth a thousand words.
A pen is worth a million guns.

Two poems out of fifteen in Moral Dury.

All of the above books by Bob are available from Amazon

Beauty

By Bob Braun

Life is Beauty

Each day begins and ends with an array of colors across the sky.
We wake from the darkness of sleep to the colors of life to love, learn, grow, and be happy.
Life gives us the ability to share our smiles and overcome the obstacles of living.
Appreciating each day and striving to improve is the essence of the beauty of life.

Health is Beauty

Strength, conditioning, diet are parts of health.
Life is finite but its quality hinges on the ability to perform the tasks of life.
We must all strive to maintain ourselves and family by becoming aware of
and then living a healthier way.
The beauty of Good Health is, it can be achieved.

Education is Beauty

Education is learning.
Learning is growth.
It's a process that should never end.
The ability to learn is installed in all of us.
The beauty of education is it can happen anywhere, anytime, at any age,
as long as the desire to improve is a way of life.

Family is Beauty

The foundation of life begins with family.
It's a must if the human race is to live on.
Parents are given the opportunity to pass on love, sharing, kindness.
It starts with patience, setting a good example, and showing love.
A strong family means a strong future, that is the beauty of family.

The Final
Art of Coaching
by Bob Braun

Normally, this section is used to provide advice or encouragement to coaches to use positive reinforcement. It is a lot easier if the players know they will receive criticism and praise in a positive manner. In this piece, I would like to touch on another extremely important matter, teaching our children a healthier way.

Many of today's children, are not getting the vitamins and minerals necessary to keep them healthy during their entire life. With the fast-food restaurants and processed foods, they are getting a high fat diet that does not provide the nutrients to build a strong immune system and help them grow. One out of four (4) children in America are overweight and most have a very poor diet. It is the responsibility of every adult to educate our youth that eating right should be a way of life. They should know as athletes it is important to feed their bodies low fat foods that are high in fiber, protein, and full of vitamins and minerals.

Coaches should instill in them the importance of eating right, plus include stretching, strengthening, and exercise in every practice. If it is running around the bases, sprinting, or having everyone run around the field, some kind of running should be used to build endurance. During practice and games, water should be available.

Make the most out of the time you have your players. In addition to perfecting their athletic skills, teach them to be healthier their entire lives. Remember, athletes use their bodies to perform their sport, and the healthier the body. the better our children and the world will be.

How Do We Know?

How do we know we are not the seed of life, whose purpose is to populate the vastness of high above?

Could it be there are no other voices and we are the first in the endless sea of space to venture beyond our world?

But first we must escape the caves of savage, greed, violence, and lust, to grow above our roots of earth to spread our branches far and wide.

It's just a matter of time before we take the virgin string of pearls that shines above each night.

Hitting Drills
and
Much More

Robert M. Braun, Sr.

What is said about ..."Hitting Drills and Much More"

Babe Ruth Bullpen

An article in the September 1997 **BABE RUTH BULLPEN** said,..."Hitting Drills and Much More," a 93-page book that, as the title implies, is much more than just a manual designed to help correct many common hitting mistakes like stepping in the bucket, over striding, and lunging. It also provides valuable information regarding the development and management of ballplayers. "Hitting Drills and Much More" is a book about keys to success.

Mike Molaro, Hopewell Valley News, ... "a book that makes people feel good about life — themselves. Enjoy the sunrises and sunsets, take time to sit back and relax, appreciate quality family time, slow down, and admire the beauty around us. That's where the "Much More" in the title comes from."

The End

Hope you enjoyed using "Hitting Drills and Much More" to help you manage young ball players. Much of the instructions on managing players and teams are beneficial tools in living a healthier life and way to teach our next generation to love life and always do their best.